AGE IS JUST A NUMBER

AGE IS JUST
A NUMBER

~ ~ ~ ~ ~ ~

Achieve Your Dreams
at Any Stage in Your Life

DARA TORRES

with *Elizabeth Weil*

BROADWAY BOOKS

New York

BROADWAY

BROADWAY BOOKS and the Broadway Books colophon are trademarks
of Random House, Inc.

Originally published in hardcover in the United States by Broadway Books, an imprint of the
Crown Publishing Group, a division of Random House, Inc., New York, in 2009.

Insert photograph of Dara, her mother, and Tessa: Photograph by Lara Stern, copyright © FoTik
Photography. All other photographs are reprinted courtesy of the author.

Library of Congress Cataloging-in-Publication Data is available upon request.

ISBN 978-0-7679-3191-5

Printed in the United States of America

Book design by Adam B. Bohannon

10 9 8 7 6 5 4 3 2 1

First Paperback Edition

*For my father, Ed Torres, for showing me what
hard work, sacrifice, and dedication mean;*

*for my mother, Marylu Kauder, for demonstrating
how to achieve your dreams while being
a knockout mother of six kids;*

*and for my daughter, Tessa, for inspiring me
as no one ever has before.*

Contents

AGE IS JUST A NUMBER

Prologue

I've been old before. I was old when I was 27 and I got divorced. I was old when I was 35 and I couldn't get pregnant. I was really old when I was 39 and my father died. But when I was 41 and I woke up in a dorm in the Olympic Village in Beijing, I didn't feel old. I felt merely—and, yes, happily—middle-aged. "The water doesn't know how old you are," I'd been telling anyone who would listen for the prior two years. Though sometimes, I have to admit, I would think to myself, *Good thing it can't see my wrinkles.*

On the morning of the 50-meter freestyle Olympic finals, I set my alarm for six o'clock. I'm a type A person, or as some of my friends call me, type A++. Basically, I'm one of those people who has to do everything I do to the fullest extent of my ability, as fast as I can. When I recently moved houses I didn't sleep until all the boxes were unpacked and all the pictures hung on the walls. I don't like to do anything halfway, and I'd set this crazy goal for myself: to make my fifth Olympic team as a 41-year-old mother. And the truth was I didn't just want to make the team, either. I wanted a medal. I wanted to win. Along the way, I also wanted to prove to the world that you don't have to put an age limit on your dreams, that the real reason most of us fear middle age is that middle age is when we give up on ourselves.

It was a pretty crazy thing to be doing, especially under the circumstances. If you've ever had a toddler or watched a parent you adore die, you'll know what I'm talking about. Young children and dying parents are truly exhausting, and I had one of each as I made my comeback. But I knew in my heart I could succeed—as long as I left no stone unturned.

The race started at 10 A.M., so I'd worked out my schedule leading up to the race. I needed to drink my Living Fuel breakfast shake at 6:15 A.M. so I'd have time to pack my roller bag—two practice suits, two racing suits, two pairs of goggles, two racing caps, two towels, and my dress sweats, in case I got a medal—before I caught the 6:45 A.M. bus over to the Water Cube. I'd then do my whole routine—wake-up swim, shower, get mashed (a massage technique done with the feet), do my warm-up swim, get stretched, and put on my racing suit—all before I headed to the ready room, where all the swimmers wait before a race. My teammates, I have to tell you, thought that roller bag was the funniest thing in the world. They were all 15 to 25 years younger than me, the ages I was at my first, second, and third Olympics. (I was already beyond their ages by my fourth.) Their bodies were like noodles, and they all carried their gear in backpacks. But I'd noticed that backpack straps made my trapezoid muscles tense up. Swimming fast, for me, is all about staying loose. So I had a roller bag. If I looked like a nutty old lady—fine.

The Beijing morning was humid and dark when I left the Olympic Village. All the other swimmers were probably still asleep. I think that the only other person awake in the Village was Mark Schubert, the National team coach of the USA Olympic swimming team. Mark had also been my coach at my first Olympics, 24 years ago. And he'd been my coach at Mission Viejo, where I'd gone to high school to train at age 16. I love Mark. He's like my fairy godfather, constantly dropping into my life at just the right time, giving me what I need, and then disappearing again. That morning he'd woken up in the Beijing predawn to help me prepare for my race. We'd come a long way together. Though he wasn't my coach in the months leading up to the Olympics, he'd taught me the discipline and the commitment to detail I now so prized. We were now going—literally—one more lap.

I rolled my bag out to the sidewalk as quietly as possible. I didn't want to wake anybody—partly because, as a mother, I knew the value of sleep. But selfishly, I also wanted my competitors to stay in their beds. The longer they slept, I told myself, the greater my advantage and the more time I had, relative to them, to prepare. Since my daughter had been born I'd been saying that waking up with a kid in the middle of the night was going to give me an edge at some point. I hoped this was it.

Over at the Water Cube the competition pool was empty, so I yelled "Good morning!" to Bob Costas, who was broadcasting up in the rafters, found my lane, and dove in. I don't usually do a wake-up swim in the competition pool, but the 50-meter freestyle is a really strategic race. Time can contract or stretch out. It's only one length of the pool—just 24 or 25 seconds—but it's also easy to get lost. If I've learned one thing from all my races and all my years, it's that the Olympics can be disorienting, and the middle of things is where we tend to lose the plot. Part of my plan for the morning was to learn exactly where I was going to be in the water at every stroke of the race. So as I swam I memorized all the landmarks, the intake jets, where all the cameras were on the bottom of the pool. That way I'd have markers in addition to the lines 15 meters from the start and 15 meters from the end. I'd know when to keep a little energy in reserve, and when to take my last breath and gun for the wall.

More was riding on this race than on any other race I'd swum. Back in Florida I had a child, Tessa, who'd one day study this race to find out who her mother was. I had a coach, Michael Lohberg, who'd believed in me before anyone else, who now lay in a hospital bed with a rare blood disorder, fighting for his life. I'd had a father, Edward, whom I'd lost to cancer just as I'd started this comeback, and who'd wanted so much for me to realize my dreams, and who I felt was with me every day.

And most unexpectedly, at least for me, I had a lot of fans.

I'm not being coy when I say the fans were unexpected. I'm saying they were unexpected because I didn't yet understand how overcoming perceived odds works—how even just attempting that can inspire people, and how the energy from those people can boomerang back to you, giving you the strength and energy you need to reach your goals. So I was surprised—deeply surprised, and also grateful—that my dream was contagious. I've always been good in a relay, but I've never been quite as strong in my individual events. I've just never been at my best when I'm swimming in front of the whole world just for myself. But now I had the support of everyone nearing or over 40, everyone who'd ever felt they were too old or too out of shape to do something but still wanted to give it a try. I had everyone who didn't want to give up. I just couldn't let all those people down. I felt they were depending on me almost in the same way my relay teammates did. We were in this together. I couldn't entice so many women and men into dreaming a little longer and aiming a little higher, and then not win.

Of course, as anyone who knows me will tell you, I wanted to win anyway. I'm pathologically competitive. I hate to lose. That's just what I'm like. If you and I were in a sack race at a field day, trying to jump across the grass with our legs stuck in bags, making total fools of ourselves, I'd still want to cross that finish line first. I'd give it everything I had. But now I wanted to win this race not just for myself. I wanted to win it for everyone who believed—everyone who *needed* to believe—that a 40-plus mom could still compete.

At 7:25 A.M. I got out of the pool and walked to the locker room to take a hot shower. The wake-up swim and the shower were both part of an effort to get my core temperature up. Everybody's core temperature drops during sleep, and that temperature needs to rise if you want to swim really fast. My plan for the remaining two hours before my race was to have my stretchers, Anne and Steve, mash—or massage—me with their feet, then swim again, then have Anne and Steve stretch me, and then put on the bottom half of my racing suit, with plenty of time remaining to lie on a massage table in the team area and listen to a bunch of rockers half my age sing a song called "Kick Some Ass." The mashing and the stretching were critical to my performance. All the other kids in the Olympics might have thought they could do their best by just swimming a little warm-up, pinwheeling their arms a few times and diving in. But not me. I was the same age as a lot of those athletes' mothers. Michael Phelps had started calling me "Mom" eight years earlier. I needed every advantage.

Physically, I have to say I didn't feel great—stiff, still not fully recovered from the prior day's semifinals. (Okay, let me pause right here and say it: I'm totally fine with aging except for the recovery time. Is it really necessary to take 48 hours to recover from a 24-second sprint?) I also felt sick to my stomach with anxiety. I'm like that, even after all these years: On the day of a big race, I feel like I'm going to throw up. I know it's part of the adrenaline surge I need in order to psych up and win. But my relationship to that surge is like an addiction. I run toward it, crave it, can't live too long without it, and then it makes me feel terrible. That prerace nausea gets me every time. I suppose when I stop feeling it I'll know it's time to call it quits and hang up my Speedo for good.

That day at the Water Cube, as my mother came over to wish me luck, and then came back to wish me luck again, I took a few swigs of Accelerade to try to calm my nerves. *Breathe, Dara, breathe,* I told myself. *It'll be over in 24 seconds.* Of course, Mark Spitz once said the really great thing about being a competitive swimmer is that your career ends quickly. He said the reward for all the long hours in the pool is that you get to retire at 23 years old. Oh, well. I was not following Spitz's schedule (though he, too, attempted a comeback at age 41). So I tried to focus instead on what I'd learned at the Olympic Trials, where I'd felt so bad just before my first heat that I was crying in the hall but swam really well anyway: *You don't have to feel good to swim fast.* I must have said it to myself a hundred times: *Don't freak out, Dara. Remember Trials. You don't have to feel good to swim fast.*

Finally, I went down to the team area and lay on a massage table for a while, listening to my iPod and watching the muscles in my quads tighten up. Then one of the coaches told me it was time to go to the ready room, which was a good thing. Because despite all my supposed maturity, for the last 20 minutes I'd been acting like an annoying kid. Every 30 seconds I'd ask: *How much longer? Is it time yet?* I couldn't stand the wait. I'd been working toward this moment for two years, or 24 years, or 41 years . . . Let's just say it had been a long time. I'd done everything I possibly could. I'd assembled the best team. I'd worked hard and smart. Now the only thing that was happening was that my muscles were tightening up.

The ready room is where they put all the athletes just before a race. I hate the place. In the ready room it's just you and the seven other girls you're swimming against, and it's either hear-a-pin-drop tense or filled with forced conviviality. When I was younger

I'd sit in the ready room with my Walkman (remember those?), and then my Discman (remember those, too?), staring at my fingernails, always keeping an eye on the trash can so I'd know where to run to vomit. That day, on purpose, I left my iPod in my roller bag. But as I ducked my head in to give the official my credentials, I could see everybody else sitting already, messing with their fingernails, or with their caps and goggles, looking sick and miserable. And the room was hot and stuffy.

For my entire career I'd been just like them—enjoying my Olympics by putting massive amounts of pressure on myself. Which is to say not enjoying the Olympics at all. But this time I felt totally blessed. *I was at the Olympics.* How cool is that? I'd sat with LeBron James and watched Michael Phelps swim. And guess what that's like? *FUN.* In just five minutes the eight of us girls were all about to do something incredible: swim in an Olympic final. By pretty much any sane person's standards, we'd already accomplished something. We were the eight fastest female swimmers in the world. We'd already won. I wanted to enjoy the experience. I wanted them to enjoy the experience. I knew we were all going out there to try to beat each other, and believe me, I wanted to win. But I felt the occasion called for a joke.

"Anybody else hot? Or is it just me?" I called out to the girls. "I feel like I'm in menopause."

I saw a smile creep across the lips of Cate Campbell, the freckly Australian redhead who up until that moment looked like she was about to meet a firing squad. I knew how she felt: like her whole future depended on the next five minutes. I now was old enough to know that there's a lot of life that happens outside of the pool. That she was going to lose loved ones and yearn for things that were outside her control. Swimming is not like real life. You can determine for yourself how hard and how well you train. You can control how you dive, how you turn, how you position your shoulders for your touch. But I knew what Cate was going through. Swimming fast can feel like the most important thing—the only important thing—in the whole world. I've been there, I've felt that. She was 16.

Maybe it was this perspective that caused me to ham it up just before 24 of the most important seconds in my life. Maybe it was nerves. Whatever the reason, I did. With just a few minutes to go before the race, all of us zipped up like sardines in our tight new racing suits, officials walked us down the hall to the rows of chairs under the bleachers. My mantra for the past two years had been to do everything all the other swimmers weren't doing—that extra vertical kick in practice, those long hours of active recovery—so I'd have something over them. But now the mom in me came out. I wanted to take care of everybody. I wanted all these girls to enjoy the event. I wanted them to relax. I knew that Libby Trickett, Cate's teammate, a really spunky Australian who'd gone into the Games ranked first in the 50 free, had just gotten married. So I asked her if she was going to have kids, and before I knew it, as 17,000 fans sat waiting for us to come out and compete, I was telling them what it's like to give birth to a child. And not just telling them. I had my feet up, as if they were in stirrups, yelling like I was in labor, just as I might have if I was sitting around my house yukking it up with my closest friends.

Then it came time to walk out to the blocks for that long, fast lap. When I got to my lane, I dried off my block with a towel, lest I slip. Then I took off my sneakers and my two T-shirts, and walked to the edge of the pool to splash my body and face. Back at the blocks, I roughed up the skin on my forearms and hands on the block's surface so I'd have a better feel for the water. Each time, just before a race, the officials blow a series of whistles—first a bunch of short bursts to warn you to get all your clothes off except your suit, cap, and goggles. Then a long whistle meaning it's time to get on your block in ready position. After that, the starting signal begins the race.

When I heard the long whistle I took my mark, with my right leg back, my left toes curled over the cool metal edge, staring down my long blue lane. I had just one word in my head, *tone,* reminding me to keep my body tight, in a toned position to knife into the water on my start. I knew everybody who dreamed my dream with me was on that block, too. But I also knew, at the starting signal, that I'd be diving into the water alone.

1

~ ~ ~ ~ ~

On Diving Back In

My favorite thing to do is to dive into a pool when no one's around. A big 50-meter pool, preferably outside, with the lane lines in. In competition, the water is so choppy you feel like you're out in the ocean, in a storm. But to me an empty outdoor pool is the most peaceful place in the world. I love diving in, breaking the surface, slipping to the other side. And once I'm in, I don't come back to the surface right away. I stay under. I turn over on my back and look up at the sky, under water. I watch the clouds, or better yet, the stars, and dolphin-kick slowly down the lane. Some people feel connected to the mountains, or to a church, or to New York City. I feel connected to the water. It's so peaceful and quiet in there.

When I was 32 and training at Stanford, after having been retired for the prior seven years, I used to climb the fence to the aquatic center on Sundays or at night, when the pool was closed. I'd climb the fence and go into the pool to be alone. One day the assistant coach handed me a key.

"What's this?" I asked.

"I know what you do," he said.

I was busted. We both laughed.

In my life, I've retired from swimming and returned to the sport three times. I retired in 1989 after my second Olympics, and then came back for the 1992 Olympic Games in Seoul. I retired in 1992 and came back for the 2000 Games in Sydney, and I retired in 2000 and came back again, to be the oldest female Olympic swimmer ever, when I competed in the 2008 Games in Beijing.

Each time I thought I was completely done with swimming, and each time I had a different reason for believing my aquatic career was over. When I retired in 1989, at the age of 22, I didn't fully appreciate swimming. I didn't fully appreciate my gift. At that point I felt sure (as only kids feel sure) that I was totally done with the sport, totally done with the water. I felt nearly allergic to the smell of chlorine, positive I'd never snap on goggles again. Swimmers are famous for this. The training is so brutal—and frankly, so boring—that when you're done, you're really done. At swim practice, when you're actually swimming, you're in a blackout world. You can't hear much. You can't see much. You can't smell anything except chlorine. So when you're finished swimming competitively, you don't even want to swim a single lap.

During the summers when I was retired, I'd sometimes spend a few weeks at my father's house in Quogue, on Long Island. He had a pool—the same pool I spent countless summer hours in as a kid—and my father and I would hang out together there. He'd sit under an umbrella reading the *New York Times*. I'd lie on a chaise lounge reading the *New York Post*. I'd finish my reading first, go for a run, shower, and then plop back down in my chair.

Most of the time I've been retired I've spent working in sports modeling or sports television. My father was quite happy to see me in the professional world. He worried about athletes who didn't build careers for themselves. His own career had been very important to him. He'd been a boss in the first downtown high-rise in Las Vegas, the Fremont Hotel, which opened in 1956. He went on to become a partner in several Las Vegas hotels, including the Riviera, the Aladdin, and the Thunderbird. His work life had been rewarding in every way. He'd made a lot of money, met a lot of interesting people, and had been sustained by it intellectually. He wanted me to find work that did those things for me, and when I was still in my twenties we both assumed that competitive swimming was only for the very young. It never occurred to either of us that I'd still be able to swim fast into my thirties, let alone my forties. No one had ever done that before. Building a career seemed like a good idea to both my father and me. Still, my father was a creature of habit. He loved routine—coffee and the newspaper every morning, Bill Hong's Chinese restaurant every Sunday night. When I'd go visit him in Quogue, he couldn't understand why I didn't want to swim in his pool.

"Don't you want to get in?" my father would ask.

"Nope," I'd say.

"Not just to swim a few laps?"

"Nope."

"Just one lap?"

"No. I really don't want to."

Sometimes the sun would be hot enough that I'd dive in to cool off. But then, much to his annoyance, I'd pop right back out and resume my place on the chaise.

~ ~ ~ ~ ~

Except, even during my first retirement, I had a plan for diving back in. I told myself I'd start swimming again if I ever got pregnant. I started telling myself this when I was 22 years old, before I wanted to have a baby or considered having one, before I knew that carrying a little creature in your belly makes you want to float around in water (warm and sudsy, or otherwise), for the buoyancy if nothing else.

I'm not totally sure why I had this plan from such a young age. Given that I'd spent so much time at pools, I'd seen a lot of pregnant women waddle over and plop in, desperate for some reduced-gravity exercise. But for me the swimming-while-pregnant plan was a little different. I didn't just want the exercise—believe me, I was going to exercise anyway. I'm an exercise nut; it's as vital to me as eating or sleeping. Some people have religion, I have the gym. I love the challenge, I love the structure, I love the sense of accomplishment as you set, work toward, and attain your goals. Since childhood I've always been extremely intense about my physical pursuits. I've never been an easygoing recreational athlete. So sometimes I think I'd planned to go back to swimming when I became pregnant because I thought, or hoped, I could swim, for just once in my life, without being so competitive and intense. (Ha! We know how that turned out!)

In the fall of 2005, I was 38 years old, 7 weeks pregnant, and throwing up more or less nonstop, when David, my boyfriend and the father of our daughter, and I started talking about swimming. David and I tend to be yin-yang. I live in my heart and in my body. He lives in his head. He's one of those people who looks at an issue from all sides before he makes a decision. He'll read up on, say, every model of new digital camera before buying one. I'm much more intuitive. I go with my gut.

At that point, pregnant and nauseous, I hadn't swum in five years. David hadn't swum in 31. He'd finished his last race on the Trinity College swim team, and like so many competitive swimmers before and after him, he'd toweled off and thrown his goggles away.

When I told David my plan to swim when I was pregnant and encouraged him to join me, he got a funny look on his face. It's hard to dive back in when you've been out of the water, even for just a day. If you're already wet and you pull yourself out to work on your starts, or use the bathroom, that's no big deal. You're happy to dive in. By that point, it feels better in the water anyway. But even just diving in at the beginning of practice, when you've been practicing every day, can take some will. Outsiders who find themselves at an elite team's swim practice always comment on that. These are real swimmers who swim all the time, a lot of them twice a day, and yet everybody's always making funny faces, hemming and hawing, stalling on the deck, trying to delay that moment of transition when they finally have to dive in.

But David had another thing making him nervous. He's 15 years older than I am. Age has a way of making new starts more difficult. I mean, compared to David I was still a kid, my hair was still wet, and my swimsuit was on a doorknob drying. Yet I could see my own questions and fears reflected in his eyes. How would it feel to swim again? Would I just be out flailing, yearning for my former self? Really, wouldn't it be better to do something else, like cycling or golf?

It's funny how inertia rules our lives, how we carve out these grooves for ourselves year by year, and the longer we're in them the harder it is to get out. It's not that whatever new activity we have in mind is, by itself, so difficult. It's just that if we leave our groove, if we do something other than what we've just been doing, we end up comparing ourselves not to what we were doing yesterday or last week (when we were already in the groove) but to what we were doing God-knows-how-many years ago. Leaving the groove is scary. What if those jeans that you haven't put on in two years won't button anymore? What if your tennis game has disintegrated in the three weeks, three months, three years, or three decades since you last played? The news might be unpleasant or it might be great, but I think it's important to know. Breaking out of a groove is like going to a high school reunion all by yourself. You're forced to compare the person you are now with the person you used to be. You have to ask some motivating questions: How am I doing? Have things gone downhill? Do I like the place my life is in right now?

So I found myself saying to David to just give it a shot, you need to wait and see how you feel. This was pretty funny, because I was really nervous myself. In almost any other circumstance I would have been the one in need of the pep talk. But David had been out of the pool more than four times longer than I had. As I now understand the math of these things, that made him over four times more nervous about getting back in.

Still, all that stuff coming out of my mouth—"Just try it. It'll be fun. What do you have to lose?"—someone should have been saying that to me.

Eventually, I won David over. He agreed to go for it, in part because there was nothing to lose, and in part because we'd fallen in love and he'd never seen me swim. David is a former doctor of mine. I'd become friends with one of his nurses, and she called me one day while I was going through a divorce to see if it was okay for her to pass my phone number along to him. He was going through a divorce as well. I was immediately drawn to David's intelligence and his honesty. Plus you know how it is with someone you love? You want to see all the different parts of that person, especially if you meet that person a little later in life. You want to look at all the photos their mothers kept of them as kids. You want to see their old haircuts, their bad fashion in high school, their first car. You want to relive their triumphs and feel their losses. You want to make up for lost time.

David had heard that a Masters swim club worked out over at Coral Springs Aquatic Complex, about ten miles from Parkland, Florida, where we lived. Parkland is in the southern part of the state, not far from Fort Lauderdale. It's flat, and hot and muggy in the summer, and really pleasant in the fall, winter, and spring, when all the snowbirds fly in. The Masters team practiced outside six mornings a week at 6:00 A.M. But before I committed to getting up that early, I decided to drive over and check out the pool.

David had told me he thought the place had an Olympic-size pool, and I had thought, *Yeah, right*. Now, I generally trust what David says. He's an incredibly smart guy, a reproductive endocrinologist. He tends to be really precise. But an Olympic-size pool must be exactly 50 meters long by either 25 yards or meters wide, and in my experience, 95 percent of the time when somebody tells you "there's an Olympic pool" that pool turns out to be 20 meters long. Or shaped like a kidney. Or, best-case scenario: The long side is 25 yards. Which for the past seven years had been totally fine, since as I've told you, the main thing I'd been doing at pools was hanging out with my family. I have 19 nieces and nephews. Small pool, no problem. Especially a small pool with a snack bar. It's fun to buy the kids ice cream cones.

So I drove through Parkland's wide flat streets, parked at the aquatic complex, and walked up the concrete ramp to check out the pool. I have to say, I was really nervous. I don't know what I expected to find—a perfectionist coach, like I'd had at the University of Florida? What I found instead was a pool that was just about as unassuming and ordinary as can be, just a big rectangular hole set into cement, with a few old bleachers on the sides and some blue and white flags overhead. Over time I truly came to love the place, its simplicity, its openness, its resistance to drama. That pool became one of the most important places in my life.

But that day only one fact about it registered in my mind: It was 50 meters.

Fifty meters is the length a real pool is supposed to be for a real swimmer, and all of a sudden it looked incredibly long. Fifty meters is about as long as half a football field, and let me tell you, if you haven't been swimming for a while, 50 meters is a marathon. You start at one end and it takes forever to get to the other side. About two-thirds of the way down your lane, you start fantasizing about your flip turn—how good it's going to feel to put your feet on a firm surface and get that kick off the wall.

But I decided to follow through on those Masters practices anyway, assuming they'd set up the pool short-course, meaning they'd string the lane lines the short way, making each length only 25 yards. The night before our first Masters practice, David and I each dug up an old suit, a cap, and a pair of goggles, and packed them together with a towel and a few toiletries in a swim bag. We set the alarm for 5:00 A.M. In the morning, we dragged ourselves out of bed and drove over to Coral Springs.

Masters is this huge association of swimmers who still train and have meets when they're older (that is, over 18; the whole sense of time in swimming is so strange). Some people just do it for the workout; some people like to race. More than 45,000 swimmers participate, in more than 1,000 workout groups and teams. The races are divided by age group, ages 18 to 24, all the way up to 85 to 89 for the men and 90 to 94 for the women. Masters really captures the essence of not being hamstrung by growing older, not giving up. That's easy for me to see now. But as a young swimmer, I'd hear about Masters swimmers and think, *Who the hell are those old folks? Masters means old. I'm not old—thank God.*

Now I was one of them.

At the aquatic center I dropped my swim bag on a bench, stretched out my traps, folded my sweats, checked the strap on my goggles, played with my cap . . . but eventually, like every swimmer before me, I had to dive in. I don't know if I'll ever get used to that sensation: feet no longer on the land, head not yet in the water. It's the ultimate state of potential, and there's no going back. It's always exhilarating and always scary. You've committed yourself. You're going in.

It wasn't an instantly blissful reunion between me and the water. For the first few laps I felt sluggish and winded, unconnected to the water I used to love. Then my stroke started coming back. The water started feeling heavy in my hands, like it's supposed to. I didn't have the dreaded sensation of just spinning my arms and not getting anywhere, like a cyclist trying to bike in too low a gear. My body, even pregnant, rode high, near the surface. My hips and my ankles loosened up, giving me a nice kick. I also remembered the straightforward nature of life in the pool. You know exactly where you're coming from. You know exactly where you're going. It's easy to state your goals. Tasks and obligations are well-defined. Life outside the water is so maddeningly full of complexity and nuance. I liked being back in the pool. The lines are clear and straight.

In fact, just five minutes after I'd been procrastinating on the deck, I felt happy to be in the pool, to feel that old sense of connection, to soak up the quiet, the peace. Even the sterile smell of chlorine felt like a relief, especially compared with the musky stink of the gym where I'd been working out that had been driving me crazy. It had been all I could do not to throw up on the StairMaster, which I'd stepped on, despite my morning sickness, almost every day. But now, just partway through the warm-up, I was feeling great—back in my body, my stroke even and rhythmic. I felt so good, so much like my former self, that I even noticed some of the other swimmers looking at me, like they were thinking, *Is she a real swimmer or something?*

But then I felt my pulse speeding up and my competitive juices flowing. So I lifted up my goggles and motioned for the Masters coach, Chris Jackson, whom I'd just met. Chris is a young guy, about 30 years old, who likes to wear baseball caps and mirrored shades, and blasts rock and roll at practice. He'd been one of the best swimmers at Coral Springs when he was a kid. He'd joined the coaching staff in 2001.

"Hey, I don't really want everybody here to know this yet, but I just want to tell you I'm pregnant," I said to him as nonchalantly as possible. "So I don't think I can swim real fast."

Chris just nodded and smiled behind his mirrored glasses.

"So, in case you're wondering why I'm not swimming fast, that's it. My doctor told me that when my pulse goes up, the baby's pulse goes up."

Chris spent a few moments standing there looking at me, with his wide-open face and his two stopwatches around his neck. He looked so young, but in the moment he was far wiser and more mature than me.

"Okay, Dara," he said. "That's great. Whatever the doctor says." Then he walked away.

Clearly, this was a question I was going to need to answer for myself: How fast was I going to swim?

But once I'd braved that first dive in, I was hooked. I went back to the pool with David the next day. And the day after that. (Okay, full disclosure: David actually had to shake me out of bed at 5:00 for the first few days. I was pregnant, after all, but I was happy to be swimming again.) I loved the feel of the water, the banter on the deck, the burble of the kicking, the slap of warm-up strokes. I appreciated the primal joy of moving through liquid more than ever. I enjoyed it even more than on those solitary nights at Stanford when I'd scaled the fence and swam underwater, looking up at the stars.

Swim practice has a reputation for being boring. I'm not going to tell you that's wrong, but swimming can be interesting, too. Working out in the water shows you the contents of your own mind. It teaches you to rein in your thoughts and come back to the present so you can focus on the small details in the pool—how you move your body, the shape of your hand as it moves under your torso, the position of your mouth when you take a breath. If your mind is in the right place in practice, you focus only on your body in the moment.

One of the most common ways to explain what makes an elite swimmer special is to say that swimmer has "a feel for the water." It has a sort of mystical ring, like the swimmer has a sixth sense for the liquid world from which we all emerged. But I think a lot of what people mean by a feel for the water is simply the ability to concentrate on how all parts of your body are moving through water at all times. Really paying attention to your body as it moves through a pool is difficult and mentally tiring. You have to keep bringing your mind back to the task at hand. For me, one of the most amazing parts of swimming again was how it forced this concentration. I was able to focus purely on what it felt like to swim, on the pure joy of the sport, on moving fast through the water, but not on winning. In practice, every turn, every breath, every kick is important. If you're half-assing your stroke when you train, you're not doing yourself any good. The whole point of practice is to perfect your swimming so that you can swim faster without thinking about it in a meet.

Until, one day in practice, some middle-aged guys started racing me.

By that point, I was showing. My regular old Speedos didn't fit anymore. I'd gone online to look for maternity swimsuits, ones that might actually cover my belly, my butt, and my boobs, all at the same time, but soon realized maternity suits aren't made for actual swimming; they're made for getting wet. So I started buying Speedos in increasingly larger sizes. I was on my second or third of these size-up Speedos when one day, at Masters practice, I noticed another swimmer, Randy Nutt, a few lanes over, looking at me to see who'd finished a freestyle set first.

Now, I loved that baby in my belly just as much as I'd ever loved anything before. I'd been trying for a long, long time to get pregnant, and as anybody who's been through that can tell you, it's a horrible, wrenching ordeal. But I was pregnant, finally and happily pregnant. In fact, I was nearly halfway through those nine big months, growing right on schedule, gaining weight according to the charts. Nothing was going to keep me from taking care of my body, bringing that baby into this world.

And yet.

I'd look over, and there would be Randy Nutt. Competitive people seek each other out in subtle ways. You know the old phrase "it takes two to tango"? Well, it takes two (at least) to have a race. We competitive people send out little signals—a look, a subtle tilt of the head that says, *Do you want to go?*—and believe me, I'm attuned to them all. One of the most blatant, for swimmers, is to see someone looking over at you during an interval, checking who's arrived back at the wall first. And there was this dude, Randy Nutt, four or five lanes over, looking over at me after each set to see what order we'd come in.

Chris, the Masters coach, noticed Randy's looking at me, and my looking back at Randy.

Chris walked over and crouched down, his stopwatches dangling around his neck as usual. Swim coaches usually have at least two stopwatches on their bodies. The whole sport is obsessed with time. As he bent down, Chris seemed to be collecting his more authoritarian coaching self, which doesn't come out at Masters all that much (unlike at high school and college practices; those coaches are all about establishing authority). Now Chris said, a little more sternly than I expected, "Dara, remember what your doctor said."

"Yeah, but . . ." I tried to explain.

"Remember what your doctor said," Chris repeated.

"Yeah, but . . . I can't. . . ."

I must have looked really determined, because Chris stood there with his arms crossed, in front of my lane, for almost a minute.

Then he bent down again and whispered to me, "Okay, go 30 seconds behind."

So I started each set half a minute after Randy. That helped a little bit, swimming offset instead of head-on. But we competitive people have our ways. Now instead of just looking over at him, I'd look over at him and try to calculate in my head where Randy had been 30 seconds before, to see if I was gaining ground. I couldn't just do my workout, forget about Randy, and relax. Sure, somebody else could. Probably almost everybody else on earth. But I couldn't. I can't ignore competition. That's just not me.

It's funny. Some of my competitive impulses have mellowed as I've gotten older. I no longer need to be the first one to get to the car. (I know, I know, you're probably thinking, *That's really big of you, Dara.* But getting to the car first was an extremely big deal for me as a kid.) I no longer need to get to the dinner table first, or be the first to answer the doorbell, or the first to say "not it" in tag, or the first to the end of the driveway on my bike, or even the first to get to practice (though I still really can't stand being last).

Yet I haven't gotten less competitive about swimming. I've

stopped swimming for long stretches, as I've told you. And I've had no interest in being in the water. But once I dive back in, as I get older, I'm more competitive than ever. And I'm not just competitive with other people. I'm competitive with myself. I know how many seconds I used to have to rest at the wall when the coach would tell us to do a set of 100-meter freestyle on 80-second intervals. I know how many seconds of rest I'd have when I was given that interval at 20 years old, and when I was given that interval at 25 years old, and when I was given that interval at 32 years old, and I want to have more seconds now. I know how long certain kicking sets used to take me. Same for pulls. Same for nearly any set you could name.

I also prefer not to be swimming at all if I can't win.

So not surprisingly, over the course of my pregnancy, Chris and I kept having the same conversation.

"Dara, remember what your doctor said."

"Yeah, but . . ."

"Remember what your doctor said."

"Yeah. . . ."

By that point, I'd done my own research and learned that doctors don't really have any idea what the pregnant body can take. Nobody's ever done a controlled study in which one group of pregnant women exercised not very much, another exercised a moderate amount, and a third exercised a ton, and then scientists compared everybody's babies. You just can't do a study like that. Too many variables, and it's unethical anyway. Who's going to risk their baby's health? The only thing doctors can tell you to do is to play it safe, and so they do. But the interesting part for me was to learn that, over the years, the amount of exercise doctors have told pregnant women is okay has steadily increased. Nobody knows the upper limit yet, and everybody's body is different. But a lot of pregnant athletes have worked out, hard, right up until the end, and their babies have been just fine. The marathon runner Paula Radcliffe ran through her pregnancy, hill workouts and all, and won the New York City Marathon 10 months after giving birth to a healthy girl. Apparently, I was going to swim through my pregnancy.

And not just toodle around in the pool, either.

No matter what size Speedo I'm wearing, no way am I getting beaten by Randy Nutt.

2

~ ~ ~ ~ ~

On Making a Comeback

I want to be really honest with you. I was not brave enough to dream this dream all at once. I didn't just wake up one day—pregnant, 38, out of the water seven years—and think, *Oh, I have a great idea! I think I'll go to Beijing and win a few more Olympic medals!*

I'm gutsy, but I'm not that gutsy. Only in the first of my three comebacks did the dream to go for a medal again appear fully formed, like a lightbulb going off in my head. At the time, in 1991, I was 24 (which probably has something to do with my bravery) and working as a production assistant at NBC Sports in New York City. I'd retired from swimming a couple of years prior but still held the American record in the 50-meter freestyle. I'd thought I'd already had a full career. I'd broken my first world record in 1982, at age 15. I'd swum and won gold medals in relays in the 1984 and 1988 Olympics. I'd also earned 28 NCAA swimming awards, the most possible, while in college at the University of Florida. So I was done. I'd retired. Each year was thought to be a huge chunk of a swimmer's competitive life span. Unless the next Olympics was very soon after your graduation, you were finished.

After completing college, I moved to New York. This was in the summer of 1990, and I got a job as a runner at NBC Sports, hoping to work my way up in sports television. About six months later, I got promoted to the very glamorous job of production assistant. My duties included logging tape—watching endless reels of footage and marking what they contained. In the spring of 1991, while I was doing this, I saw on my screen and heard through my headphones that the Olympic ice-skater Brian Boitano, who was then 27 years old, was making a comeback. I hadn't been in the pool in about a year and a half, but I thought to myself, *Comeback! Wow, I should make a comeback.*

I'd never really considered a comeback before.

I sat with the idea in my head for about an hour. The notion of swimming competitively again felt like one of those kids' toys, a small capsule that you put in a bucket of water and five hours later it's grown into an enormous dinosaur. I could not sit still. I kept thinking about Brian Boitano and his reentry into his sport. (It didn't hurt that Nicole Haislett had also recently broken my American record in the 100-meter freestyle.) Finally, five o'clock rolled around and I went home and called a coach named Mitch Ivey at the University of Florida. We hadn't worked together directly when I'd been a student and swimming there, but he was a two-time Olympic medalist, and he'd coached my sister, Lara, for a while in California. I'd heard good things about him.

Once you're out of college in the United States, there's no formal system for athletes to train. Some countries, like Germany and China, have national training programs. But not the United States. Here you pick a club, probably at your alma mater, and pay to be a member of the team. Natalie Coughlin, the most versatile female swimmer in the United States, still swims at the University of

California at Berkeley. Same routine for Aaron Peirsol at the University of Texas, and Ryan Lochte at the University of Florida. If I was going to train for a comeback, it was going to be at the University of Florida. I didn't consider going anywhere else.

When I first called Mitch, I was a little bit tentative on the phone. "Hey, Mitch," I said. "I'm thinking about swimming again. And about coming down there and training with you."

Mitch was happy enough to hear from me. Then he said something that surprised me, though it shouldn't have. He said, "Well, I need to know if you're over your eating disorder."

"What?" I said.

"You know what I'm talking about."

He'd called my bluff. I'd been bulimic when I'd swum in college and at the 1988 Olympics. In fact, I'd been bulimic for the past five years. I'd thought I'd kept it a secret, but if Mitch knew, pretty much the entire Florida swimming community must have known.

~ ~ ~ ~ ~

I don't blame my college coach, Randy Reese, or the swimming program at the University of Florida, for making me bulimic. I could have, and probably would have, developed an eating disorder anywhere, and I'd chosen to go to college at the University of Florida because Randy had a reputation for being innovative and tough. At the time the University of Florida, the University of Texas, and Stanford University were the best swimming schools in the country. I ruled out Stanford—too academic. Between Texas and Florida I'd chosen Florida, because Randy was so demanding. (I was also worried that the Texas swim team would lose its coach during my college career, and I was right.) I wanted a coach who would help me hone my work ethic. I wanted a coach who would push me to build more stamina and speed. I'd visited Florida and watched the Gators practice only once before I joined the team. At the time they were tapering—swimming less than usual so they'd be rested for a big meet. So when I enrolled I didn't know what Randy's practices were normally like.

Arriving in Gainesville for my freshman year, I was one of 13 new female swimmers. Only seven of us finished the first season. The night before our first practice, a bunch of the older swimmers took us rookies out to dinner. They started telling us stories about Randy—about the grueling dry-land workouts in the University of Florida stadium, the treading water we'd have to do with five-pound weights over our heads. I figured they were hazing us like pledges at a fraternity, making Randy's practices sound worse than they were. But this was not hazing. At our first practice, Randy made us swim 7,000 meters (about twice as much as I was used to). He threw a chair across the deck. After that we went to the stadium, where we ran up the stairs and down the bleachers. Randy didn't dole out many compliments. He just gave instructions. If you didn't perform, he yelled.

Randy was willing to try anything to make his swimmers strong, and I wanted to be strong for him. Some days Randy had us do kicking drills with tennis shoes on our feet. Other times we pulled football sleds on the stadium infield, even when that infield was dry and the temperature was 100 degrees. We lifted weights, we jumped weighted jump ropes, and most indelibly seared in my mind, we did something he called "wheels." Wheels were performed on the stadium ramps. They horrified my mom. We'd tape our hands so we didn't get blisters, and then lie down in push-up position, parallel to the ground, with a two-by-four with wheels the size of skateboard wheels attached to each end under our knees, so our toes almost dragged on the ground. The task was to pull our bodies with our hands up the stadium ramps while remaining prone. There were a lot of skinned knees.

Randy also weighed us before practice. He thought lean swimmers would look intimidating on the blocks. His target weights for us were reasonable; at 5'11½" I was supposed to be less than 152 pounds. But if you didn't make weight, you had to join what Randy called "the breakfast club." That meant you had to swim 11 workouts that week instead of nine. Those workouts were at 5:30 A.M. on Tuesday and Thursday mornings, the only weekday mornings we typically had off.

I was desperate to please Randy. If he wanted me to look lean and intimidating, then I wanted to look lean and intimidating, too. I craved his approval. The tiniest compliment out of his mouth made my day. So I ran extra stairs. I did extra wheels. I spent more time jumping weighted ropes. I wanted to be what he wanted me to be.

In the process, I grew addicted to exercise and developed an eating disorder. I would have done anything not to join the breakfast club. And I did.

I exercised, hard, seven days a week. If I skipped a day I felt horrible about myself, fat and lazy. Randy weighed our team on Mondays. So Sundays, even though we didn't have a scheduled workout, I'd run four miles and starve myself. A few other girls on the team did this, too. They'd starve themselves Sundays. Then, after weigh-in Monday, we'd all be so hungry that we'd go binge in the bathroom. (We didn't want Randy to see us chowing.) Eventually, Randy caught wind of this routine, so he started weighing us twice a week, assuming we couldn't starve ourselves on Sundays and Wednesdays, too. But twice a week wasn't too much for me. I just rose to the challenge.

My eating disorder began in earnest one day during my freshman year when I was eating in the dining hall with a bunch of girls. A few of us were complaining about eating too much and feeling too full, when another athlete (not a swimmer) at the table piped up and said, "If you eat too much, all you have to do is get rid of it."

This was not something I'd ever thought about. I'd grown up a massive tomboy. The weigh-ins before practice had made me newly obsessed with my weight.

The girl who knew how to "get rid of it" walked into the bathroom. Three or four of us followed. She stuck her fingers down her throat and she made herself throw up.

It took me five years to get over that lesson, five horrible obsessive years. Soon I was regularly purging after meals, too. In hindsight it's hard to believe how quickly it happened. Here I was, one of the most promising swimmers in the country and the current world-record holder in the 50-meter freestyle, and I was bulimic. I knew this was terrible for my body and my swimming, but I couldn't stop myself.

The worst part of my bulimia was its psychological effect. Sure, I had no energy in the water, and my face was bloated and my hair and skin were dry. But the real problem was that I lost my mind. I was extremely dark and moody. All I could think about was food. I'd see a girl having dinner and my crazy thoughts would start looping. *How can she be thin? How much does she work out? How can she eat whatever she wants and when I look at food I gain weight?* I was particularly envious of the guys on the swim team. Their bodies were so long and lean. I was still growing through my first year in college. I added an inch in height. I was scared that I wasn't fully finished with puberty. I didn't want to add inches to my hips and chest, too.

Pretty much all I thought about during college was what I ate, what I wanted to eat, what other people ate, what I'd need to do to get rid of the calories I'd ingested, how much exercise I got, and how I would look in my swimsuit when I mounted the blocks. Somehow I managed to win those 28 NCAA All-American awards, but the truth is my college years were a very hard time. I did manage to have a few lighthearted moments. For a while I had a conehead lizard named Melvin. I dated a guy on the swim team. I used to love teasing the kids in the Greek system, whom I'd call Susie Sorority and Freddy Frat. One day a Susie Sorority in my statistics class made fun of my hairy legs. I was growing out my leg hair, like all female swimmers did, so that shaving would have a bigger impact at the championship meet at the end of the season. But this poor Susie, she teased the wrong girl. I really let her have it, which I must say felt great. I had dreams much bigger than Kappa Kappa Gamma—dreams of winning medals at future Olympics. Or at least I had those dreams when I wasn't obsessing about food.

The worst was pizza, about which I developed a huge fear. When our team flew to other schools for swim meets, Randy would bring on the plane a huge stack of pizzas. (He also threatened to bring the scale.) I wanted to eat that pizza so badly, slice after slice, but I felt I couldn't. There was nowhere private on the plane to throw up. So even though I had been swimming, running, lifting, and doing wheels, burning Lord-knows-how-many calories, I'd take just one piece and nibble around the edge. I was trying to fool my teammates into thinking I was normal. Really, I was dying inside.

A few times during college I sought out help. My sophomore year, I told an orthopedist I knew that I thought I had bulimia. Eating disorders weren't his thing. To his credit, he brought me some literature, but I just used it to excuse myself. One pamphlet had a checklist of what to look for in a person who suffers from bulimia. Yellow teeth? No, I didn't have yellow teeth. Cuts on my knuckles? No, no cuts. I figured I must be okay.

~ ~ ~ ~ ~

At that point I'd already competed in one Olympic Games, in 1984 in my hometown, Los Angeles. I was 17 years old at the time, and my age showed. I qualified for only one event, the 4 × 100-meter freestyle relay. The 50-meter freestyle was not yet an Olympic event. I wasn't very happy about this. The 50 was then, and still is, my race. I held the world record in the 50-meter freestyle at the time.

To give you an idea of what I was like at age 17: I was still such a kid, so propelled by impulse and energy, I actually threw myself into a picture with President Ronald Reagan. He'd come to talk to all the American Olympic athletes, but only the team captains were invited up on the stage. I wasn't a team captain, but I still wanted to get that snapshot. So after the President spoke I tossed my camera to a friend and jumped up next to him on the stage. At that point in my life, I was into getting my picture taken with celebrities. When my favorite band, Men at Work, was in Los Angeles on tour, I started cold-calling fancy hotels, asking for the lead singer, Colin Hay, until one operator finally connected me to his room, at which point I slammed down the phone and drove with my sister and a friend to his hotel to stake him out. We must have waited in my car for over an hour, listening to my Men at Work tape and flipping through a scrapbook of Men at Work clippings I'd snipped out of *Tiger Beat* magazine. Then Colin Hay's limo pulled up. I started screaming, "Oh, my God!" but once I actually got out of the car and onto the sidewalk, I pulled myself together enough to get an autograph and a snapshot. At the 1984 Olympics, I thought I'd pull off the same thing with Ronald Reagan. It never occurred to me that Reagan's Secret Service men might see an unauthorized teenager as a security breach. When I jumped on stage, they all reached for their guns.

Partly because the 1984 Olympics were in my hometown, I maintained the illusion that the Olympics were just another swim meet right up until the end. I slept in the Olympic Village with all the other athletes, but the magnitude of the event did not catch up with me until just hours before the preliminaries for the 4 × 100-meter freestyle relay, my first race. That morning I went with the other swimmers down to the athletes' tent, where we all waited before our events. Right before my race, my good friend Rowdy Gaines was swimming in the preliminaries of the 100-meter freestyle. So I lifted up the bottom of the athletes' tent to try to see him.

This was not wise.

I didn't see Rowdy's friendly face. I saw 17,000 people sitting in the stands.

Those of you who spend your Saturdays in muggy arenas already know this: Most swim meets do not draw big crowds. The bleachers are usually filled with parents and bored siblings and other swimmers messing around. It takes many hours to get through the countless heats of every event. There's never anywhere near 17,000 people. One hundred and seventy would be pretty good. I couldn't believe I was supposed to walk out there and swim in front of that crowd. I'm not shy. I generally love attention. But this was too much. I freaked out.

My body flushed hot. I had to go to the nurses' station. I had a full-on panic attack. The nurses placed ice packs all over me.

Then, 20 minutes later, it was time for my relay. Over the years I've learned how to collect myself quickly for big races, but at age 17, I did not fare well. I swam so poorly, in fact, the coaches hoped to pull me from the final that evening and substitute Jill Sterkel, the poised 23-year-old team captain. But that afternoon Jill did something I have never forgotten. She took me back to our dorm in the Olympic Village, where she insisted we do puzzles and watch soap operas so that I could calm down. Her objective was to prepare me mentally to swim well in the finals of the relay. In the process, she taught me how to be a good teammate. That's a lesson I'll carry with me for the rest of my life.

So thanks to Jill, I swam in the finals of the relay. She did not. I even swam my 100-meter split in 55.92 seconds, a personal best. (Swimmers almost always swim faster in relays than in individual events; there's more adrenaline and it's easier to time the start. Relays have what's called a "moving start"; you get to watch a swimmer moving toward you before you dive. Individual races—and the leadoff leg in relays—have a "flat start"; you have to react only to the starting signal.)

Our relay team won gold by nearly a second. I returned to the Westlake School for Girls, very proud and ready to be back in high school. Still, whenever I think of the 1984 Olympics, the first word that comes to mind is "scary."

~ ~ ~ ~ ~

Before I started training for the 1988 Olympics, in my junior year of college, I consulted a nutritionist about my bulimia, but I wasn't ready to give up my eating disorder, so she wasn't much help. The big concession I made in preparing for the upcoming Games in Seoul was to stop making myself throw up just prior to big meets. To compensate I ate even less than usual, so I can't imagine it helped much.

That year, at the NCAA championships, with the help of assistant coach Skip Foster, who was coaching the sprinters, I won the 50-yard freestyle, the 100-yard freestyle, and the 100-yard butterfly. I was named the College Swimmer of the Year. But I was inconsistent mentally, and I didn't swim my best at Olympic Trials. The 50-meter freestyle, my specialty, was finally an Olympic event, but I finished fourth at Trials and so did not earn a spot on the U.S. roster in that event. Olympic rules dictate that only two swimmers per country can swim in each individual event. (This rule went into effect in 1984, and prevents any one country from sweeping the medals.) The rules, however, are slightly different for the 100-meter freestyle, in which the top six finishers make the team. The 100-meter freestyle is part of three events: the individual 100-meter freestyle race; the 4 × 100-meter freestyle relay (in which four swimmers each swim 100 meters of freestyle); and the 4 × 100-meter medley relay (in which four swimmers swim 100 meters of one of the four different strokes: backstroke, breaststroke, butterfly, and freestyle). The top two finishers in the 100-meter freestyle are on the roster for the individual 100-meter race. The other four help flesh out the relays.

At Olympic Trials for 1988, I finished third in the 100-meter freestyle, so initially it looked as if I'd only be swimming the 4 × 100-meter freestyle relay again. But a week after Trials, the winner of the 100-meter freestyle, Angel Myers, was disqualified for failing a drug test. This bumped me up to second in the 100-meter freestyle, meaning I'd have a spot in the individual 100-meter freestyle. I'd probably swim on the relays, too.

The 1988 Olympic Games in Seoul were excruciating for me. I couldn't figure out what or how to eat. In truth, those Games were a little tough on the entire American swim team. There was a strong anti-American sentiment at the Games. Even the big stars, like Matt Biondi, did not start the meet as strongly as they might have hoped. Our relay teams did well enough: We won a bronze medal in the 4 × 100-meter freestyle relay and a silver medal in the 4 × 100-meter medley relay. But my individual 100-meter freestyle race did not go off as planned. Going into Trials, I was ranked number one in the world in the 100-meter freestyle, but I swam poorly at Trials and I swam poorly again in Seoul. At the Olympics I placed seventh in the 100-meter freestyle, a huge disappointment to me. An East German, Kristin Otto, won both the 50-meter and

100-meter freestyle. (The East German swimmers won nearly every event; many of the swimmers were later discredited for doping.) Near the end of the Games, I overheard Kristin tell a reporter, in what I considered to be terrible sportsmanship, "I thought I'd have more competition out of Dara Torres."

That felt like a knife in my back, and in my heart.

~ ~ ~ ~ ~

I finally got help for my bulimia in 1990, the year after I graduated from college. By that point, my mother knew something was very wrong. I was living in New York and had that production assistant job at NBC. When I'd go home to visit her in Sun Valley, I'd push my food around my plate. I'd eat only when no one was around. I'm sure my mother noticed that, too. She'd read about Karen Carpenter, the singer who famously died of anorexia in 1983. My mother begged me to see a doctor she knew in New York. Finally, in January of 1991, I consented. I was tired of all my secrets, tired of feeling ashamed and weak.

To this day, I'm not sure if my mother had spoken with the doctor in advance, but that doctor asked me every medical question you can think of. "How much alcohol do you drink? How many hours do you sleep a night? Have you noticed any changes in appetite?"

She also asked, "Have you ever made yourself throw up?"

I said "no," so she kept on asking her questions. "How frequently do you have sex? How frequently do you empty your bladder?"

Finally, she finished. She listened to my heart, checked my blood pressure, and felt around for lumps in my breasts. I put on my clothes, started to leave, but even before I'd exited the waiting room, I started feeling sick. I'd lied to this woman, right to her face. I turned around and knocked on her office door.

"Sorry to bother you," I said, "but I just wanted to talk to you about one thing. I lied to you on one of your questions."

"Which one was that?" she asked.

"That I don't make myself throw up. I do. I think I have bulimia."

She invited me back in and gave me the name of a psychiatrist. I told her I would call.

I didn't want to see a shrink. I wanted to get better by taking a pill. I wanted my eating disorder to just disappear. But I went to see the psychiatrist a couple of times a week. We talked about my dad, his focus on food, my competitiveness, my desires to win and to please. The therapy, I have to admit, did help a little. I started throwing up less. But I knew that this wasn't the complete answer. Then, a few months later, when I was at work at NBC, I saw that tape of Brian Boitano announcing his comeback and I had that brilliant idea of making my own comeback. A big part of the motivation to swim in the Olympics again was feeling as though I had been mentally unprepared in the 1984 and 1988 Games. So I fudged things for Coach Ivey when he asked me if I was over my eating disorder. I really wanted to swim again, and I felt confident that the goal of winning another Olympic medal would help me quit vomiting for good.

"I'm pretty much better. I've been seeing a psychiatrist . . . ," I told Mitch.

Thankfully, he took me at my word. He agreed to allow me to come down to train, as long as I kept seeing a psychiatrist.

Within a week, I'd found a shrink in Florida and moved to Gainesville to train.

People ask me all the time what it takes to wage a successful comeback. And I have a simple answer: You have to want to keep winning, and to want it badly. You have to be determined to move closer to reaching your full potential, instead of letting yourself slip farther away.

When, in 1991, I decided to train for the Olympics again, I didn't consciously think that I had unfinished business in the pool. I just knew I wanted to swim again. I missed competition. I missed the speed. I missed the focus. I missed funneling thousands of miles of training into one or two lengths of the pool.

It's not that I didn't care about my life in New York or my television job. I did. I loved them both, and I was very grateful for them. But the dream of earning another Olympic medal was just so overwhelming. I knew I could swim faster than I had in the 1988 Olympic Games. Besides, once a big idea like that takes hold of me, I tend to act on it quickly and not look back. I don't think about the negatives, or entertain doubts. I just move forward. I focus single-mindedly on my success. I suppose it's blindly optimistic, but it's also effective. I believe in hard work, and my ability to do it. I've met very few people who want to win more than I do.

Now, comebacks are complicated. You may have decided it's time to reassert yourself back into your sport, but everyone else might not be ready for you. Swim teams often have Byzantine dynamics. Swimmers train as teams and race as individuals. Typically, everybody's nice and congenial on the surface, and the chatter stays pretty light on the deck, but the emotional needs of all the team members are not always in line.

It takes great maturity to navigate team dynamics. I like to think I've gotten better at it as I've grown older. But in 1991, I was 24, and I didn't pause to consider how my presence back in the pool would affect the other swimmers. I just packed up my apartment in New York and moved to Florida, where I'd last trained. I didn't imagine the Gators swim team was going to throw me a homecoming party, but I wasn't quite prepared for the cold shoulder I received, either. This was pretty ironic, given that I was absolutely no threat to anybody. I was still recovering from my eating disorder and all those years of mistreating my body. I felt terrible in the water, heavy and stiff. I felt like I couldn't pull.

From my perspective, that first day back in the water in Florida was a disaster. I felt worse swimming that day than any day before or any day since. I know it might sound strange, but when a competitive swimmer feels bad in the water, the water doesn't feel too heavy and hard to move, it feels too light. You feel like your hands are slipping through thin liquid instead of grabbing viscous chunks. The sensation is that your arms are spinning but you're not getting anywhere.

None of that mattered to the other swimmers. All that mattered was that I had retired. I had left the game. I was supposed to be gone. Particularly cool to me was Nicole Haislett, the University of Florida undergraduate who'd broken my American record in the 100-meter freestyle earlier that year in the 1991 World Championships. Nicole had a really cute young smile, a great tan, and bleached-out blond hair, but she was tough in every way you could imagine—physically tough, mentally tough. You could not psych her out. So when I walked out on deck and slid off my shorts and flip-flops, Nicole did not greet me with smiles and hugs. But I didn't want to apologize for my presence. Sorry? I wasn't sorry to be there. There was nothing to do and little to say. We both dove in.

Over that year, against long odds, Nicole and I became close. Neither of us did much else besides train. We weren't roommates, but our lives were virtually the same. We both went to practice, came home, ate, watched TV, and slept, and then went to practice, came home, ate, watched TV, and slept again, all in the same day. Sometimes Nicole would make me dinner. Occasionally, we'd see a movie. But mostly, if we weren't in the gym or in the pool, we slept. Swim training in an Olympic year is very intense and insular. You can't even talk to your teammates most of the time you're practicing. It's just you and your body, focusing on your head position, your pull, and your kick, lap after lap after lap.

As I had hoped, the goal of swimming in another Olympics motivated me to stop vomiting. I quit cold turkey once I arrived in Florida. I didn't want to repeat the experience I'd had in 1988, when I'd stood on the blocks at the Olympics less than perfectly prepared.

I'd only given myself one year from the time I moved to Florida until Olympic Trials, the meet that would determine who would be on the 1992 Olympic swim team. During that time I met Jeff Gowen, a handsome, athletic sports producer eight years older than me, who would become my first husband. We'd been introduced when he was coordinating the filming of a Florida Gators football game, and I was instantly impressed by how nice he was to everybody, even the guys pulling the wires needed for the cameras on the field. On our first date, Jeff and I stayed up all night walking around Lake Alice in Gainesville. I fell in love with him quickly, but I was so laser-focused on my swimming that year that I barely saw him at all.

Trials in 1992 were in Indianapolis. I knew my times would have to improve in that meet if I was going to make the Olympic team, but I had confidence that they would. I came in fourth in the 100-meter freestyle, swimming that race in 55.48 seconds, earning myself a spot on the relay team. But I finished fifth in the 100-meter butterfly, posting a time of 1:00.30 seconds, and a disappointing eighth in the 50-meter freestyle, with 26.15 seconds. I couldn't believe that I couldn't put together a faster race in my trademark event. I chalked up my slow touches to my age. I was 25 years old, thought to be ancient in those days. The girls on the team called me "Grandma." They also elected me captain, an honor that seemed to reflect their opinion that I'd soon be gone from the sport.

In Spain I swam in only one event, the 4 × 100-meter freestyle relay. I was disappointed not to be swimming in any individual events, but at least nothing embarrassing happened—no freak-out in the preliminary, no choking in the final. Jeff, the sports producer I'd been putting off, came to Spain and watched me swim. Because of menstrual pain, I almost passed out on my way to the podium to collect my relay medal. But I had done it. Mission accomplished. I'd come out of retirement and won a gold medal. Now I could put my Olympic ambitions behind me and move on with my life.

After the Games I moved back to New York—and into an intense, heady courtship with Jeff. The two of us had a fantastic time together when Jeff wasn't in a horrible mood. I kept thinking those moods, and the fights they caused, would disappear when we were more settled. Only a couple of months after I returned from Barcelona, Jeff took me to the airport and told me to cover my eyes as the two of us boarded a plane. He took me to Gainesville and back to Lake Alice, where he sank down on one knee and proposed. By that point I'd told everybody, in no uncertain terms, that I was done swimming forever. I'd swum in three Olympics. I'd set world records. I'd represented my country and seen the world. I'd never stood on an Olympic podium by myself (which of course I wanted to do), but I tried to push that thought out of my mind.

I was getting married, and I told myself I was satisfied with what I'd achieved. In New York I stashed my Olympic medals under my bed. I didn't like people asking me about them, because then I'd have to admit that I'd won them only in relays. So I stored my medals safely out of sight, where they collected dust and turned black with tarnish.

3

~ ~ ~ ~ ~

On Making a Comeback
Yet Again

My 1992 comeback was not my last. I guess, with my medals under my bed, I should have realized I had unfinished business in the pool. But like I said, I did my best to push those feelings aside.

My father offered me a choice between a down payment on a house or a big New York wedding, and I picked the Vera Wang dress and a reception at Le Club in Manhattan. Jeff and I said our vows in May 1993, just nine months after the Barcelona Olympics, and the truth is, at the altar, I knew I was probably making a mistake but I was too young, afraid, and stubborn to call the marriage off. Jeff first scared me with his temper about a month after we met. He'd flown back down to Gainesville to take me out to dinner, and he'd yelled at me for eating crackers before our date. I never visited him in Connecticut in the lead-up to the 1992 Olympics because I couldn't break my training schedule. So I made excuses. I thought Jeff's temper would improve once I stopped training or we were engaged or married.

Unfortunately, I was wrong. Jeff and I fought horribly during our engagement and into our marriage. He screamed and I cried. He'd attack me over petty things, like what I hung on our walls. One major source of contention was the prenuptial agreement my father insisted Jeff sign. At a time when most newlyweds would still be honeymooning, Jeff and I started seeing a couples counselor in Connecticut, where we lived. Among our more upsetting, and more ridiculous, fights, was the one we had after a fun day of snowmobiling in Sun Valley. I encouraged Jeff to shower first, he refused, and then he grew irate and cancelled our dinner date, aggrieved over how much hot water I'd used. (I'd taken a bath in only three inches of water in order to conserve for him.) Our final fight came in April 1995 when Jeff yelled at me for how I styled my hair. Up to that point, I'd always tried to take the blame for whatever was bothering him—yes, I should have let you shower first; no, that needlepoint shouldn't be on the wall. But finally I realized that even if I took down the needlepoint Jeff would continue to find fault. The stress of our relationship made me relapse into bulimia for a time. We split up after just two years.

Divorced and 28 years old, I moved back into New York City. It felt good to be in Manhattan again. My life was primarily dedicated to relaunching my abandoned career. I tried reading the news as a local anchor, but that wasn't for me. Next I tried hosting sports lifestyle shows for ESPN2 and the Discovery Channel, and this worked out much better. I'd joke around with golfers and other athletes on camera. At one point, I beat the world champion at street luge—an insane sport in which you lie on your back on an oversized skateboard and race downhill.

About a year before my divorce, in 1994, I'd been asked to be the first female athlete model in the *Sports Illustrated* swimsuit issue. I'd been hoping to be put in sexy little bikinis, because I was used to always wearing Speedos, but the stylist outfitted me in sporty one-pieces. Still, that job led to many modeling opportunities. Mostly, given my background and my physique, I did sports modeling, illustrating workout moves in magazines like *Glamour* and *SELF*. This was so much fun for me. I'd been such a jock growing up that it was a kick to have someone do my hair and makeup, and style me to look really feminine. But I also found the work frustrating. I was used to succeeding in competitions by having some talent and then working a thousand times harder than everybody else. With modeling, either they like your nose or your legs or your face or they don't like your nose or your legs or your face. I found the auditions, called "go-sees," very stressful.

In those days, for exercise, I worked out at the Reebok gym, played hoops, and ran and cycled in Central Park. Each time I had a go-see, I'd wake up in the morning, work out, and then take the subway downtown to sit with a bunch of gorgeous women in a room. There I'd start asking myself, "What on earth am I doing here?" I don't have high cheekbones or emerald green eyes.

But I had a nice life. I didn't swim at all, which drove my creature-of-habit dad crazy. He and I would still have those same conversations when we'd leave the city and go to the house in Quogue on weekends.

"Don't you want to swim some laps?"

"Nope."

"Not just one lap?"

"Not just one."

Then, in the spring of 1999, New York senator Al D'Amato asked me if I'd join his niece at the U. S. Nationals swim meet. I'd met the senator through some acquaintances of my dad. Senator D'Amato had always been gracious to me. Nationals happened to be on Long Island, not far from my father's house in Quogue, so how could I say no? At that point, I was so distant from the sport that not only had I not swum laps in seven years, I hadn't been to a swim meet in that long, either. I'd even flown to Atlanta for the 1996 Summer Olympics and watched no swimming at all. I kid you not. I watched gymnastics, badminton, and track and field. But I never once went to the pool.

For Nationals, I took a train out from Manhattan to Long Island with a friend. Walking onto that pool deck did not exactly rekindle my love of the sport. I remember being hit by the wet, heavy smell of chlorine and hating the way it made me feel. The backs of the female swimmers looked way too big. Everywhere I saw bags under swimmers' eyes from too many early-morning workouts and not enough sleep.

I hung around all day, watched some races, saw some old friends, and encouraged Al D'Amato's niece.

"I'm so glad that I don't swim anymore," I whispered to my friend as we left.

I figured I'd never go to a swim meet again.

~ ~ ~ ~ ~

A few months after that Nationals meet, early in the summer of 1999, I was out to dinner with a date and some friends—not swimming friends, just regular friends—and the subject of swimming came up. After dinner, my date and I stood on the subway platform, waiting to get the 6 train from Hunter College to Twenty-third Street to go to a Meat Loaf concert at Chelsea Piers. (What can I say? I grew up with four older brothers.) As we stood there, my date asked, "Have you ever realized that when the subject of swimming comes up you get this gleam in your eye?"

I thought he had to be out of his mind. "No, no," I said, "that's not true. I'm so sick of swimming."

"No, seriously, you do," he said.

"Well, maybe that's because I was in the sport for so many years."

"No, it's something else. Do you ever think about a comeback?"

"A comeback? Ummmm, no. I had a comeback. And I'm 32. And I have not touched the water in seven years."

Before the concert started, he brought it up again. "Really, you should think about swimming."

"Look, it's not going to happen," I said. "Just drop it."

Well, he dropped it, and I couldn't get the thought out of my head.

I became obsessed. I dreamed about swimming all night, and in the morning, to shake it off, I put on my headphones and went running in Central Park. I planned to run my regular six-mile route around the perimeter. I was partway through, cruising along, thinking about whether 32 years old was just sort of old or actually over the hill, when a woman who must have been 70 or 75 years old ran right past me—fast. All of my competitive energies came roaring back. I picked up my pace. If she didn't have to be old at 70, I certainly wasn't going to be old at 32.

I ran home just as quickly as I could.

Back at my apartment, when I caught my breath, I called Richard Quick. By that point in my life, I knew pretty much everybody in the swimming world. Richard was a very experienced coach, part of the American Olympic coaching staff in the 1984, 1988, 1992, and 1996 Olympic Games. He was one of the best.

Richard was then coaching the Stanford women's team, and you can always tell when he's in the room because he smells of sunscreen. He didn't answer when I called, so I just said, "Hey, it's Dara. I need to ask you something. Just give me a call when you get a chance." Then I sat by the phone. It was about noon in New York, nine in the morning in California. I figured Richard was still at morning practice.

I sat by the phone all day, but he never called.

The next morning, as always, I got up and went to the gym. A few minutes after I returned, Richard finally called. We chitchatted for a few minutes. Then Richard said, "I know why you're calling."

"You do?" I asked.

"You want to make a comeback."

"How can you tell that from a message on your machine?"

"I don't know—it was something in your voice."

I paused. Then I said, "So, what do you think?"

Richard's wise opinion was that I should sit with the idea for a few days to make sure I was serious. "Think about it and call me back," he told me. "Meanwhile, I'll talk to the team and see what they think."

It was hard for me to just sit there thinking. (I'm not the world's greatest sitter, as you might have guessed.) So I called my mom. A former model, she has always been very enthusiastic about my swimming, even if at times she didn't show me directly. When I was a kid, she'd come to every meet and videotape my swims. When each meet was over, she'd find me and give me a hug, looking collected and composed as ever. Only later, when I watched the tapes she'd made, did I realize that every time I stepped on the blocks she'd start screaming and cheering for me at the top of her lungs, too overcome by emotion to care that the video camera was recording her voice.

My mother had since moved from Los Angeles to Sun Valley, Idaho. I said, "Hey, Mom, I'm thinking about coming back. . . ."

Her voice lit up. "What flight are you coming on, honey?"

"No! I'm not talking about coming to Sun Valley. I'm thinking about making a comeback. In swimming."

She hung quietly on the other end of the line for a moment. I could hear her covering the mouthpiece and talking to my step-father, Ed Kauder, who'd been right alongside my mother, driving me to practice and watching me in meets, since I was a kid. Ed had been in the family since I was six years old. He was one of the best tournament tennis players in his age bracket. He had always encouraged me to swim. While my mom had the mouthpiece covered, I figured for sure she was going to return to the line and say, "What, are you nuts? You're 32 years old. Stick with your television and modeling career!" But she didn't. When she got back on the line, she said, "That's so wonderful, sweetheart! You should follow your dreams and go for it!"

I think she was really surprised, but my mother is amazing. She always supports her children. Plus I think Ed talked her into it.

A few days later, I called Richard back. By that time he'd talked with the girls on the Stanford team, including the lightning-fast sprinter Jenny Thompson, who'd graduated four years earlier but still trained with the team. Richard said everyone, including Jenny, was enthusiastic about having me come train with them.

So that was it. I was making comeback number two. I just had to shut down my life in New York. That meant telling my modeling agent, Dieter Esch, and telling my dad.

~ ~ ~ ~ ~

I decided to tackle the easier one first, so I took the subway down to Gramercy Park to find Dieter.

Dieter is a bear of a German guy, and the head of the agency I worked for, Wilhelmina. He'd been a real mentor to me, steering my career where it needed to go—namely, into sports modeling. I was so sure of myself I just walked into his office and said, "I have to tell you something. I'm leaving to go to California. I'm not going to be modeling for the next year. I'm going to make a comeback in swimming. I'm going to try to swim in the 2000 Olympic Games."

All over his walls were classic modeling posters. Blown-up faces of beautiful girls with perfect noses and perfect teeth and perfect hair. I had thought for the past few years that I wanted to be one of them, to be the perfect girl in the picture, the way my mother had been. I keep a modeling photo of my mother in a frame in my house—she's such a natural. In it she's standing in the corner of what appears to be some old alley in Tuscany. She's wearing a long black dress with a slit up to the knee, black shoes and black gloves, and the dress is sleeveless, so you can see her beautiful arms. My mother is the master of looking beautiful and sexy without giving anything away. She looks fantastic: feminine, strong, mysterious, and gorgeous.

I don't know if I was drawn to modeling for the competitiveness with the other girls, or for the excuse for keeping my body in top form, or if I was just trying to live up to the standard set by my mom. Whatever the case, that dream was quickly overpowered by the idea of another gold medal. I was certain I could still swim fast.

But Dieter was not very enthusiastic about my comeback plan. In fact, he was downright grumpy. He said, "There's no way you're going to make the Olympic team."

Negativity like that reduces some people to tears, or makes them retreat, but not me. It makes me want to prove people wrong. So I just looked at Dieter and said, "You don't think I'm going to make the team, huh? What's our bet?"

That seemed to crack him. Dieter then walked around his desk, gave me a hug, and said, "If you make it to the Olympics, I'm coming."

The next obstacle was my dad. At that point, my father was living in New York and all my other siblings were either in Sun Valley or Florida. My father and I had dinner alone together every Sunday night. My father was a very strict man, and very old-fashioned. He did not change his opinions easily. I loved him dearly, but it was very hard to tell him things.

In New York, my father and I were each other's only family. We'd grown very close. In general this meant the world to me, but it was also making me nervous about telling him my plans. Even more than my mother, my father wanted me to meet a man, settle down, remarry, and start a family. I was 32 years old, after all—to my father's mind, past due for motherhood. My four older brothers and my younger sister all already had kids. And if I wasn't going to have kids yet, I should at least be building my career.

The night I planned to tell my father about my comeback was the last Sunday in June 1999. We met at Bill Hong's Chinese restaurant on the Upper East Side. My father and I had been eating there together for over ten years, and for the 20 years before that my father had been eating at Pearls, a different Chinese restaurant where some of the same waitstaff had worked. My father loved dining out. Like a lot of Jewish men of his generation, his life revolved around meals and he took food very seriously. My plan for the evening was to put my news out there as early as possible, so I could try to enjoy what I knew was going to be my last Sunday-night dinner with my dad for a while, or at least try to get him to understand why I felt compelled to swim again.

Shortly after we arrived, our favorite waiter walked over with menus and poured us tea. I'd known this waiter since I'd graduated from college. My father must have known him for 30 years. I decided I would tell my father about my comeback while we were figuring out what to eat. But just as my dad was opening his menu, the waiter said to me, "You still swim?"

All I could think was, *Why is he asking me this, on tonight of all nights?*

I said, "Nah, I don't swim anymore."

"You young. You should still swim!" the waiter insisted.

I couldn't believe this was happening. For a split second I figured I could play it to my advantage, or at least use the waiter's comments for a smooth transition along the lines of, "Well, Dad, I've been meaning to tell you something." But then my dad chimed in and practically shouted, "Young! She's not young! She's 32! She shouldn't be swimming. She needs to stick with her career!"

And I thought, *Oh well. I guess I'm not telling my dad tonight.*

After a miserable meal, I went home and wrote my father a letter. I had already bought myself a ticket on an early flight the next day to California, so in the morning, before dawn, I dropped the letter off with my father's doorman, with careful instructions to give it to my father when he came downstairs for his coffee and newspaper, as he did every day. The letter explained that I'd decided I wanted to see how much farther I could go in swimming. I told my father I wanted to make the 2000 Olympic team, and that I hoped he'd support me in that dream. My plan at that point was to be in California for a week. I would look for a place to live near the Stanford campus and then go to Los Angeles to shoot a few last infomercials for the fitness company Tae Bo. A week later, over the July Fourth holiday, I would return to New York to pack up.

I flew to California. Three days passed. I called my dad.

"Well, I read your letter," he started out, flatly.

"Okay," I said.

"I don't mind you doing it, under one condition."

"What's that?"

"That you continue somehow to polish up on your career in television: take a class, take some lessons . . ."

"Okay," I said.

That was it, our whole conversation. I didn't entirely understand my father's attitude about my swimming, but I was relieved to have his support. I didn't even stay out in California long enough to find an apartment. I was so eager to start training that

I just flew back east, packed up my belongings, and shipped my boxes to Richard Quick's office.

~ ~ ~ ~ ~

My comeback for the 2000 Games was only slightly more premeditated than the one I'd made in 1992, and I paid the price. In hindsight I understand why it stirred up tensions. But as I've said, once I make a decision, I just go for it. I don't lie awake nights hemming and hawing. I move fast. I rush in.

Now, I can sit in my rocking chair and tell you that it's better to take your time, to let your comeback emerge, to make sure you're training with the right plan and the right team. But that would be disingenuous. That's not how I live my life. I did luck into the perfect situation for my third and most recent comeback, in 2008. In my second comeback, for the 2000 Games, I had a great coach and I swam with great swimmers, but still my presence on the pool deck triggered a lot of intense emotions, not all of them positive.

At first everything felt so smooth and so right. When I landed back in San Francisco, three weeks after I'd first called Richard, I rented a car and drove south on Highway 101. I love that drive. It's really amazing, especially when the sun is shining and the air is clear. That day, the light made everything look new and full of possibility, with the mountains on one side, the bay on the other, and the blue July sky overhead and the sun streaming through the windows. I cranked up the music loud and sped south toward Stanford, feeling that storied California renewal, absolutely certain I was in the right place.

For the first few nights, I slept at Jenny Thompson's house. Jenny, like me, had been on the 1992 Olympic team; we'd won gold medals together on the 4 × 100-meter freestyle relay. At those Games she also held the world records in the 50-meter and 100-meter freestyle, soundly beating me in my strongest events. Now Jenny was 26 years old, not quite an old lady like me, at 32, but not a kid either—like the Stanford undergraduates, the youngest of whom may well have still been in diapers when I swam in my first Olympics in 1984! Much to my relief, when I first arrived at Stanford, the mood on the pool deck was friendly and receptive. Even better, I felt good in the water—I had stayed very fit in the intervening years, and I no longer had an eating disorder to get over, as I'd had in my previous comeback.

The only bump I could foresee was that Richard, along with all his swimmers, was leaving in a few weeks to compete in Nationals, the biggest swim meet in the country in non-Olympic years. Whoever made the National team would then fly with Richard directly on to the Pan-Pacific Games. This meant I'd have to do much of my early training alone, but I was not concerned. I was plenty motivated.

Before Richard left, he took me out to lunch so he could give me a series of workouts to follow while he was away. He brought a legal pad on which he had handwritten my practices. His primary concern was that I not do anything too hard—just lay down a base, keep my heart rate under 150, not go too fast. (You can imagine how closely I followed that.)

Then the conversation turned to my goals. Each season, every coach has this discussion with each of his swimmers. Together they decide how high to aim. The best coaches pick something just at the edge of what's possible for each of their swimmers, then coach those swimmers into swimming faster than they ever thought they could. When I first arrived in Palo Alto, I didn't really know what my 32-year-old body was capable of, and I didn't want to overreach, so I decided to downplay my ambitions. I told Richard I just wanted to be an alternate on the Olympic relay, nothing more. When I imagined this conversation in my mind before talking to him, I'd tell Richard I wanted to be an alternate on the relay and he'd then say, "Oh, c'mon, Dara! You can do better than that! We've got to aim higher!"

But that's not what happened.

When I told Richard I wanted to be an alternate on the relay, which required just placing in the top six in the 100-meter freestyle at Olympic Trials, he agreed. Later he told me that he was worried that at my age I might not have the strength to make the Olympic team at all. But Richard is a very positive guy. He kept his message upbeat and his fears to himself.

So he just said, "Great, let's get on that relay!" and handed me my legal pad of workouts.

I was not exactly thrilled.

As it turned out, Jenny was the only girl on the team who made the Pan-Pac Games. After Nationals, Richard and the team let her fly on, and when Jenny met us back at Stanford, four weeks after she first left, I was feeling great. By that point, I was swimming in the lead lane at practice, a surprise to everybody, including myself.

Before Jenny had left for her two big meets, she'd introduced me to Robert Weir, her strength-training coach. During her absence, along with my swim training, I spent at least an hour a day in the gym, lifting weights. Robert had me doing fairly standard exercises—bench presses, leg presses, reverse upright rows, incline dumbbell curls, pull-ups, and straight-arm pullovers. But he designed his sets incredibly well, and he kept me interested. By the end of September, when Jenny returned, I was the strongest I'd ever been. Under Robert's guidance, I'd built up to doing pyramids of bench presses—eight reps at 135 pounds, six reps at 155 pounds, four reps at 175 pounds, and three reps at 195 pounds. My leg press pyramids topped out with three reps at 600 pounds.

Earlier in the summer, before her trip, Jenny had asked me to be her dry-landing training partner. I'd said yes. We'd been spending either two or four hours a day together in the water (depending on whether we had a single or double practice that day), and at least another hour together lifting in the gym.

But by the end of that first week back together, tension started to build.

It wasn't a verbal thing—we were still both overtly friendly. But the vibes started turning bad. Just a month earlier, when I'd walked onto the pool deck, Jenny was hands down the best. Now her position was less clear. Compounding matters, Jenny didn't seem to like that I was asking for extra attention from the coaches. One of the first things Richard had said to me, at my first practice, was, "Dara, we don't swim like that anymore." So I asked him to help me with my technique, to help me update my stroke.

Many people think of freestyle as the easiest stroke, because pretty much everybody who can swim can do it. But it's hard to do perfectly. Tiny adjustments in technique can make a huge difference in speed. That day, Richard told me I needed to keep my head down and look at the bottom of the pool, instead of looking ahead. (It's harder than it sounds to keep your head down and straight while your shoulders are moving up and down.) He also wanted me to change the percentage of time I spent on each of the freestyle's three phases.

The freestyle stroke cycle can be split into three parts: the catch phase, the propulsion phase, and recovery phase. The catch phase is where you grab the water in front of you with your hand and sweep it down under your elbow. The propulsion phase is where you push the water down along your body. The recovery phase is where you take your hand out of the water and bring it out in front of your body again. For the most part, my actual stroke was still good, but Richard wanted me to make one major adjustment. He wanted me to take my hand out of the water by my waist, instead of following through and exiting my hand near my thigh, shorting my propulsion phase. That might sound strange, since the propulsion phase is where most of the power comes from in freestyle. But by exiting my hand sooner I was making my stroke more efficient. By the time your hand is stretched down to your leg and your arm is almost straight, you've lost most of the ability to push backward on the water. If my hand left the water sooner, I could bring my opposite arm into the catch phase sooner, spending more time on the parts of my stroke that made me move fast.

Each aspect of swimming presents its own particular challenges. Breaststroke, which noncompetitive swimmers often think of as even easier than freestyle, is extremely technically difficult. The slightest mistakes in form can really slow you down. Butterfly, which many noncompetitive swimmers think of as nearly impossible, is actually all about maintaining a rhythm. Sure, it's physically demanding; but it's probably easier to master than noncompetitive swimmers believe. Backstroke is a lot like freestyle. The key is keeping your head back and completely still. For this reason, many swimmers prefer to do backstroke indoors. It really helps to focus on something on the ceiling, just like it helps a dancer to focus on the horizon while doing turns. But backstroke isn't just freestyle flipped over on its belly. The hand motion underwater is completely different. In freestyle, the hands move straight down and underneath the body during the pull. In backstroke, the hands stay away from the body as the elbows come down the sides.

While training under Richard I started forming my personal philosophy of leaving no stone unturned. Each day before practice, I ducked into Richard's office to see if I could look at the workout sheet. Sometimes he would show me, sometimes he wouldn't. But I wanted to see it, if possible. I wanted to do everything I could to improve my performance. I didn't drink alcohol. I didn't drink coffee. I always got enough sleep. I wanted to do everything in my power to be thoroughly prepared.

In November, just four months after returning to swimming, I posted a lifetime best in the 50-meter freestyle in a short-course event in Maryland that was part of the swimming World Cup. The race itself wasn't a tremendous deal, as winning short-course meets (swum in 25-meter pools) doesn't always translate into success in more conventional long-course meets (swum in 50-meter pools). That extra turn really changes the dynamic. As Mark Spitz once said to a short-course champ challenging him in a long-course meet, "This is swimming, not turns." Still, that personal best at the World Cup was a big milestone for me. It was proof that, at age 32, I wasn't just trying to catch up with my former self. My technique was improving. I felt great mentally. I was more committed than ever to performing every drill in practice to the best of my abilities. When I was young, I was a natural athlete, but undisciplined. In my prime the pressure of performing up to other people's expectations sometimes got the better of me. Now that I was older, I felt capable of making the most of my talent—focusing more when I was in the pool, and taking better care of my body. Age, for me, was a positive factor. Physically I felt strong, and mentally I was more mature.

Then, a month later, in December, just five months into my comeback, our whole team flew to San Antonio, Texas, to race in the U.S. Open, an important event. This time I didn't just post a personal best. I won the 50-meter freestyle, beating the American record holder, Amy Van Dyken, as well as my teammate Jenny. This was the first time I'd ever beaten Jenny in a meet. I touched the wall in 25.29 seconds, 0.36 seconds faster than she, and 0.4 seconds faster than I had when I'd set a world record in the 50-meter freestyle in 1983.

I flipped up my goggles and looked at the scoreboard. I felt terrific—confident that last month's personal best wasn't just a fluke. It was now clear to me, and to Richard, that we could aim higher than just getting me a spot as an alternate on the relay team. My 2000 comeback was taking shape. The only problem was that Jenny was supposed to be the best swimmer on our team. Jenny was supposed to be the best female sprinter in the country, perhaps even the best female sprinter in the world.

My beating her in the 50-meter freestyle was more than our increasingly fragile relationship could bear.

~ ~ ~ ~ ~

In the lead-up to the 2000 Olympics, Jenny and I were training in the same events: the 100-meter butterfly, the 100-meter freestyle, and the 50-meter freestyle. I'm sure, before I arrived at Stanford, that she pictured the two of us training alongside each other, and herself swimming faster than me. My best times in 1992, when I was 25 years old, were slower than her best times in 1999, when I was 32. Yet when my speed improved to match hers, Jenny's feelings changed. We raced each other—battled each other—in practice every day.

After the U.S. Open, Richard had requested that all of his swimmers fly directly to Colorado Springs for a training camp at the Olympic Training Center. I followed his directions, as did one other swimmer, Misty Hyman. Before Jenny joined me there, she first flew back to Stanford along with all the other girls on the team. Over the next few days, unbeknownst to me, Jenny held a series of meetings. When my teammates arrived in Colorado Springs, they'd made a decision: I was getting too much attention. I should be kicked off the team.

During our first practice together in Colorado, Richard pulled Jenny out of the pool to talk. It was a crisp early-December day, veering toward the holidays. I wasn't feeling too joyful, but I was hoping we could make some peace. Before practice Jenny had refused to make eye contact with me. When she walked back on deck with Richard, she looked happier and more relaxed. I took this as a good sign.

But the next thing I knew, Jenny was in her lane and Richard was waving me out of the pool.

"Please don't tell me what I think you're going to tell me," I said as I approached him on the deck.

"Just go get dressed. I need to talk with you," he said.

I knew in my gut what was coming. Ten minutes later, Richard and I were driving around in the team van. I was sobbing before he opened his mouth. Richard told me that he had to ask me to leave the team. He said the other swimmers didn't like how much time I was requesting from the coaching staff. More than that, the competition between Jenny and me had gotten out of hand. We were damaging each other in practice both mentally and physically. Our competition was unhealthy and counterproductive for our training. We approached every practice like an Olympic final. No matter the set, we raced. My mind was always tracking where Jenny was in the water. I was constantly pushing myself to beat her, and she was pushing herself to beat me, too. This is not the way that you build speed. If all you care about is being the fastest all the time, you can't train tactically. Training to sprint and sprinting get confused, and this sacrifices the quality of both.

The reason for this is that sprinting is largely anaerobic exercise, the term used to describe activities that require too much energy in too short a time for the oxygen in the bloodstream to keep up. When the oxygen in your bloodstream can't keep up, you have to burn the carbohydrates in your muscles, a process that releases lactic acid and causes your muscles to hurt. By contrast, lower-intensity exercises, like jogging, cycling, and endurance swimming, are largely aerobic. You get most of the energy you need by burning the oxygen in your blood. Swim races over 200 meters are primarily aerobic, while shorter races are primarily anaerobic, though both short and long races are both. Aerobic combustion is about 19 times more efficient than anaerobic combustion, but for a sprinter aerobic combustion cannot supply the necessary fuel quickly enough.

The optimal training for anaerobic activities, like sprinting, is different from the optimal training for endurance sports. In the pool, sprinters need to do more high-intensity workouts and less volume. The goal is to create both more strength and more capacity in the muscles to process lactic acid. If too much lactic acid builds up in the muscles, you get a condition called acidosis. Acidosis is the main reason sprinters' muscles get fatigued after 20 or 30 seconds. It's why I find swimming 100 meters so much harder than swimming 50 meters. It's why those longer sprints are harder to recover from, too.

A real sprint breaks down your muscles. If you want to improve, after you sprint you have to let your muscles recover and build back up. Really high-intensity workouts should only be undertaken once or twice a week. Within workouts, maximum effort needs to be followed by plenty of rest. Unlike endurance, which is built slogging through massive numbers of meters day after day, speed is built on frugality. In some ways, speed is like money. If you don't spend it wisely, if you just go for broke day after day, you'll soon find it gone.

Swim coaches talk about "visiting speed," occasionally and at precise times. But Jenny and I didn't have firm enough control over our own competitive instincts not to visit speed at practice nearly every day. Perhaps it's unrealistic to put any two closely matched sprinters in a pool and think they're not going to race. Whatever the case, we raced. We raced a lot. A local newspaper called the dynamic between us at practice "a war and a fiasco." I can't say that's entirely wrong.

So now Richard and I were driving in a van around Colorado Springs, and he was telling me I needed to go. I was 32 years old. I'd been married and divorced. My siblings all had kids. I couldn't help but feel I was in the middle of a swimming drama more suited to high school. Not that I didn't understand Richard's decision: He'd been training Jenny at Stanford first. What hurt most were the small indignities. I was told that I needed to move my belongings out of the Olympic Training Center dorms. I was told I could not practice in the Training Center pool when Jenny was around. I was also told that I could train only with the assistant coach.

I moved into a hotel room in Colorado Springs and stayed for a few days. I was reluctant to let go of Richard. I'd come so far with him so quickly, and I refused to give up on performing well in the 2000 Olympic Games. I called a few other coaches I knew, including Mark Schubert, to discuss my possibilities, but the Olympics were only nine months away. I didn't want a new coach and a new training program. I had a plan. It was working. I wanted to stick with it.

I remained in Colorado Springs for a few more days. I worked out, avoiding the girls in the weight room, and I swam, avoiding the girls at the pool, but mostly I just cried. Eventually, I got my wits about me and said, "Screw this." It was almost Christmas. I flew to Florida to be with my dad.

My father and I didn't talk about Jenny. We just kept each other company. I swam a little at a pool nearby, and a few days later Richard called to ask when I was coming back to California. I told him I thought I'd be out in a week to collect my stuff and move down to southern California to train with Mark Schubert. But when I was in Palo Alto, Richard asked me to meet him at the pool. There he told me he thought he'd found a solution: Richard would coach me in the mornings in any empty lane at the Santa

Clara Swim Club, just 20 minutes south of Stanford. I could train there, without him, with a dozen or so men on the U.S. National team in the afternoons. If Jenny and the Stanford team weren't at the Stanford pool, he would train me there.

He didn't tell Jenny about this plan right away, and when she found out, she didn't like it. But Richard felt his primary obligation was to train the best American Olympic swimming team. That meant training both Jenny *and* me.

Richard worked me harder in that Santa Clara pool than I'd ever been worked before, though he did it with a plan. Mondays and Wednesdays were high-intensity workouts. Tuesday and Thursday practices were all about recovery. Fridays and Saturdays we determined each week, according to what my body needed most. But those high-intensity workouts were something else. Sometimes Richard would have me do 30-minute sets of fast 50-meter sprints. Again and again, up and down the pool, he'd pace the deck, screaming at me, as I swam all out. Sometimes I'd do 20 in a row, averaging 28 seconds each. At the end I'd hang my head in the gutter, trying not to throw up.

Richard also had me do endless drills, each focused on building one small piece of a perfect stroke. For balance Richard had me stand on two kickboards in the water, one under each foot. He'd throw tennis balls. I'd have to catch them without falling off. We also spent hour upon hour on my head position. When I'd learned my freestyle stroke in the 1980s, I'd been taught to swim the stroke leading with my face, with the waterline hitting my forehead. Now Richard wanted me to keep my head straight down, eyes staring at the bottom of the pool, with the waterline hitting my crown. This kept my neck higher and longer, and it improved my posture as I swam. Even now I'm amazed by how much speed in the water depends on tiny variations in form. The turbulence you create in the water with your own body can really slow you down.

That July, at Olympic Trials in Indianapolis, I set a new American record in the 100-meter butterfly, swimming the preliminaries in 57.58 seconds. But even there, swimming against Jenny again, I got taken down by my competitive drive. In the finals of the 100-meter butterfly I made the mistake of looking for Jenny. When I turned my head, I botched my rhythm. She beat me by .08 of a second, which really burned, though we both made the Olympic team in that event.

In the 100-meter freestyle at Olympic Trials I touched second to Jenny as well. I won the 50-meter freestyle. (Jenny scratched this race.) At age 33, I was heading to the Olympics in Sydney in five events: my three individual races plus the 4 × 100-meter freestyle relay and the 4 × 100-medley relay. During Trials, my father, then 83 years old, sat in the stands, wearing a baseball cap with my name on it. It was the last time he saw me swim.

Sydney was an incredible site for the Games—such a beautiful city, right there on the water—but in Australia I faced not just Jenny but Inge de Bruijn. Inge, a 26-year-old Dutch sprinter, had set eight world records leading up to the Games. She was huge and dominant, and worse, she was swimming all my events. I took a bronze to her gold in my first event, the 100-meter butterfly. (A Slovakian swimmer named Martina Moravcova took silver.) I also took a bronze to her gold in the 50-meter freestyle. (A Swedish swimmer named Therese Alshammar took silver.) Inge took gold in the 100-meter freestyle too, and in a bizarre twist of fate, Jenny and I *tied* for bronze. (Alshammar took silver again.) At the end of the 100-meter freestyle, I looked up at the board. I just saw the 3 next to my name and I thought, *Cool, I won bronze.* Then I saw another 3 next to Jenny's name, and I couldn't believe it. Many spectators in the stands in Sydney broke out in gasps and laughter. The story of our rivalry had been all over the press. At that point in Olympic history, only one other swim race had ended with a tie: My American teammates Nancy Hogshead and Carrie Steinseifer had tied for gold in the 100-meter freestyle in 1984.

The irony of the two of us together on the same step of the podium was lost on no one. Standing up there together listening to Inge's Dutch anthem, "Het Wilhemus," had to be some of the most frustrating minutes of my life. Interestingly, Olympic races are actually timed to the thousandth of a second, but the official clock only counts hundredths. (In 1972, the Olympic Committee decided that an irregularity in the pool wall could cause the swimmer in one lane to touch a thousandth or two before the swimmer in another, so they stopped that level of hair-splitting.) About a month after the Games, Mark Spitz called me. "I was there in Sydney when you swam," he told me. "I know who won the tie." According to Mark, my name flashed up first on the scoreboard and Jenny's flashed up below mine, and this meant my time was faster. I'd like to think so, but the truth is I don't know if Mark is right.

After winning both relays (which Jenny swam in, too), I left Sydney with five medals, including three from individual events. As I've told you before, I'd always hated when people asked me how I won my four Olympic medals and I'd have to say they were all from relays. At age 33, I'd accomplished more than I had at age 17, or age 21, or age 25. But I was also exhausted to my core. I didn't even warm down after my last relay. I just toweled off, put on my clothes, accepted my medal, and broke into tears walking away from the pool to get drug-tested one last time. I'd competed in those Olympics every day in my head for the past 13 months. Now I was done. I'd succeeded. I didn't know what to do with my life.

On my way out of the arena, a reporter approached. "Will we see you back at age 41 in 2008?" he asked.

I didn't even have the energy to smile.

I just said, "That's the dumbest thing I've ever heard."

0124 069 N N N N 690 PZI0
008 2000035??-1 [...] 2H11 109

4

~ ~ ~ ~ ~

On Motherhood and Other Forms of Cross-Training

I didn't have a team when I first started my comeback for the 2008 Olympics, because as far as I knew at that point, I wasn't making a comeback, I was having a baby. I guess you could say that even though Tessa was *in utero* she and I were a team. She was my partner, my motivator, and my reality check. After the first few weeks, she and I didn't feel like waking up too often at 5:00 A.M. to make it to the 6:00 A.M. Masters practice. So most days I'd let David go ahead to train with the Masters team. Then I'd have Chris Jackson, the Masters' coach, e-mail me a workout, which I'd do in the late morning or early afternoon when I met my friend Barbara at the pool.

Barbara Protzman, my training partner, was a serious Masters swimmer about 10 years older than me. She was tall, with chlorine-bleached hair and a deep, year-round tan. Three or four times a week, I'd meet Barbara at the pool. She'd bring fins. I'd bring my increasingly large torso. And together we kept swimming right up until the end. I waddled out there in my oversized Speedo as I passed the seven-month mark, then the eight-month mark, and into the homestretch. One of the things Barbara found funniest about swimming with me while I was pregnant was that I'd still "deck change"—just wrap a towel around my ballooning body and change into my swimsuit right there on the pool deck. (Swimmers are nearly naked all the time, so we aren't the most modest people.) At that time, Barbara was the perfect training partner for me: experienced, reliable, fun, and not too competitive. I couldn't have handled an aggressive training partner once I had an enormous belly. Pregnancy did slow me down some, but I still wanted to win.

More days than not, after swimming I'd go lift in the gym. This wasn't part of a comeback plan, nor was it intended to be showoffy or macho. I'm just an extremely physical person. I love to exercise. It's who I am. It's important to me that my body look good and that I be physically strong. Exercise also keeps me feeling sane and calm. So it's not surprising to me that I stayed extremely fit through my pregnancy. Some people find that amazing, but I'm amazed by women who work at their jobs straight up until just before they deliver. Or by women like my mother, who had me, and then my sister, when she was already wrangling four or five kids.

Also, as you've no doubt guessed, I'm not very interested in slowing down. Not in my car, not in my body. Not in any area of my life. I hate being cut off or delayed by other drivers on the road. I like to swim, run, bike, and travel at the fastest possible speed. So even with Tessa in my belly, I kept swimming, fast, always listening closely to my body, always staying tuned to when I stopped feeling good. I'm a big believer in that, too: paying attention to what your own body is telling you. We're all different. Our bodies all feel different things. Exercising while pregnant felt good to me. So that's what I did. I swam and lifted weights right up until the end.

By March I'd grown so enormous that pretty much everybody at the pool had started coming up to me and saying, "Aren't you going to have that baby yet? You look HUGE." And to be totally honest, I was pretty ready to have that baby myself. I'm impatient. I'm also tall and lean, with narrow hips. I gained 35 pounds and Tessa stuck out of the front of my body like a watermelon. It was especially strange to have my protruding belly in the weight room. Weight rooms, despite the fact that lots of women use them, still feel like a guys' place. I like the male energy, I like working out with men, but while I was weight training and pregnant I kept looking over my shoulder. I felt self-conscious. I appeared to have stuck one of those half-sphere Bosu balls under my oversized T-shirt.

~ ~ ~ ~ ~

One thing I learned from being a pregnant athlete and then an athlete-mom is that when it comes to women, sports, and child-bearing, often people's first reaction is to say, "No, you can't." You can't do those exercises. You can't go that fast. You can't win that race. But most of the time that negativity is not based on fact. It's based on ignorance or fear. So I chose to do my own research. I wanted to learn what my own body could take.

All Olympic athletes are extreme people. We're outliers on the curve. The gymnasts are tiny, and the basketball players are huge, and the swimmers are really flexible with big flipperlike feet. (Mine are size 10½.) Plus, like many elite athletes, I wasn't putting in eight hours at a desk or in a classroom, then trying to maintain a super-high level of fitness in a few spare hours after work. I had the luxury of being sponsored by Toyota and Speedo. Being in top form was central to my work. As an athlete-mom, I swam five days a week for two hours and did strength training four days a week for 90 minutes after my swim practice. I would have been just as happy to work out more, but that amount of exercise made my body perform best.

One afternoon, when Tessa was a toddler, I took her to our regular playground after I'd completed my swimming and weight training for the day. A mom named Africa, whom I saw there sometimes, ran up to me and said, "Oh my God, I was just at the pool signing my kids up for swimming and I saw some articles about you! I had no idea you were such an accomplished athlete."

She was being very sweet, and I was flattered. This was before the 2008 Olympics, and pretty much nobody had any idea who I was. But I have to say my first reaction was, "Are you kidding? Look at my shoulders! You think a mom who's not a professional athlete would ever have time to look like this?"

Near the end of my pregnancy, an increasing number of people wanted to make sure I wasn't doing too much, but not everybody. About a week before my due date, I swam midday with Barbara Protzman, and when I finished I found Michael Lohberg, the head of the swimming program at the Coral Springs Aquatic Complex, standing at the end of my lane. Michael was born in Germany and is in his late fifties. He has graying hair, a warm smile, and just enough of a belly that his swimmers are always teasing him that he really needs to be exercising more. I didn't know Michael well at that point, but I had a good feeling about him. I could tell he was easygoing and direct. Or, I should say, I'd *had* a good feeling until he opened his mouth at the end of my lane and asked if I would swim in a Masters meet he was hosting at Coral Springs in four weeks.

The meet was just before Mother's Day. Michael stood there in his shorts, sneakers, sunglasses, and polo shirt. He had a funny way of both having a sparkle in his eye and looking slightly put out. That day he told me that a reporter from the South Florida *Sun-*

Sentinel, Sharon Robb, had called him to see if he might be able to get me to swim so that she could write a Mother's Day piece on me. I could see the story already: the old Olympian, the new baby, feel-good stuff. Michael was keen on the idea, too. He thought this might make for some nice publicity for his swim club.

Now, I'm all for helping other people out. I've been very lucky financially in a sport in which it's nearly impossible to train at an elite level and hold down a job. Many swimmers juggle complicated arrangements involving roommates, burritos, odd jobs, and small sponsorships in order to stay in the sport. Given my good fortune, I try to be generous with my resources and my time. I talk to kids' groups and speak about worthy causes to help raise awareness and research funds. My father died of colon cancer, so I speak about colon cancer. I had trouble getting pregnant, so I speak about infertility. I was bulimic, so I speak about eating disorders. I'm even the face of this blood-clotting disorder I've got called Factor Five Leiden.

What I'm trying to say is: I'm all for giving back to my community and even using my status as an Olympian to do so. I've signed autographs at a restaurant to help raise money for autism research as part of a kid's bar mitzvah project. But even by my standards, Michael's request was a little out there. I mean, hadn't he looked at me?

In case the absurdity of this situation isn't clear, let me paint the scene. I am in a Speedo. I am nine months pregnant. My belly is so large that I cannot look down and see my toes. There are only two possible scenarios a sane person could imagine. One, I will be even more pregnant at this meet in four weeks, absurdly pregnant, and in completely laughable condition to swim. (You try swimming with a basketball in your suit.)

Or two, I will be having a baby at some point between now and this Masters meet, meaning I'd probably show up in some horrible hormonal postpartum funk, with a newborn screaming or dangling off my breast, and my loose belly hanging in front of me like a deflated inner tube.

I didn't know Michael all that well at that point, so I wasn't quite sure what to think. I felt fairly certain he wasn't flat-out crazy, based on our few previous interactions. We'd met for the first time even before I'd started swimming again, when I walked up to the desk at Coral Springs Aquatic Complex to find out about their programs. The swim club, as I've said, is pleasantly simple. You walk up the front stairs, there's an office, and in that office is a desk behind which sits a nice woman named Gail.

"Um, yeah, hi," I sputtered at Gail, not totally clear on what I was doing. "I guess I just wanted to find out about your swimming programs."

Gail looked up. "What kind of group do you think you should be swimming with?"

"Oh, I don't know. Maybe with the elite kids?"

The look on Gail's face got a little bit quizzical. I didn't look like a kid at all, and I was nearly green from morning sickness.

"Do you have much swimming experience?" she said.

"Yeah," I said, "I've swum a decent amount."

"Have you done any meets?"

"Sure, I've done some stuff."

Finally, Gail got sick of my beating around the bush and said, "Look, let's do this. If you have any meets or accomplishments the coaching staff might want to know about, why don't you write them on this piece of paper, and I'll make sure they get to the right place."

She slid me a piece of paper, and I thought, *This is pretty funny, but what the heck?* I wrote down "4 Olympic Games, 9 Olympic medals, World Championship, Pan-American Games, National

Championships, 28-time NCAA All American." Then I wrote my name and phone number.

When I finished, I folded the paper. Gail was on the phone, so I placed it on her desk.

On my way home, I wondered what was going to happen when someone read my note. It had been a really long time since I'd been an anonymous swimmer. The swimming community isn't all that big. Since I was 10 years old, I'd always known all the coaches and I'd decided for myself where I wanted to train. But I'd been retired for 12 of the past 14 years. I was ancient history.

A few hours later, my phone rang.

"Is this Dara?" Michael Lohberg asked with his German accent. I hadn't ever met Michael, but I knew his reputation and name. He had coached swimmers at six Olympic Games, including a bunch at which I'd competed. He'd even trained his own wife, Birgit Lohberg-Schultz, for the 200-meter freestyle in the 1988 Games in Seoul, where I'd swum, too. Now, at Coral Springs, he trained elite high school kids year-round and, leading up to Olympic years, he trained whoever showed up (as long as they passed his muster), usually a couple dozen college and post-college swimmers from across the globe, many of whom wound up at the Games.

Michael chuckled at me in an affectionate way. "Why didn't you tell her who you were?"

"Oh, I don't know. She didn't recognize me, and I felt dumb pressing my case."

He chuckled as if he could understand. "Come find me tomorrow at four and I'll show you around."

The tour Michael gave me around the swim center didn't take long. In addition to the 50-meter pool, the place had a 25-yard-by-25-meter pool, kiddie pool, and diving well, and everything was clean and well-maintained. At that point, Michael had zero interest in training me. He evidently wanted to watch me for a while, to see how serious I was about swimming again. (He didn't yet know I was pregnant.) So I stayed a Masters swimmer for the next year, swimming under the direction of Chris Jackson, the rock-and-roll-playing Masters coach. Occasionally, Michael would come look at my stroke and mutter a few Teutonic words under his breath. But for the next six months he and I barely spoke at all.

Then, there he was, in early April, oblivious to my huge belly, trying to sell me on his Mother's Day meet.

Now, I'm about as hard-core a fitness buff as you're going to find, but in terms of what to expect from a pregnant or postpartum body Michael was way out in front of me. Yet he also seemed confident and comfortable about his absurd request, and I liked that in him. Against all reason, I found myself telling Michael that I'd ask my doctor if I could swim in a race in four weeks.

I went to my obstetrician, Dr. Zafran, the next day, but the question seemed too ridiculous to raise. And I couldn't bring myself to ask it at the next appointment. Or at the next one after that, either.

By that point, I was going to Dr. Zafran every other day, gearing up for Tessa's birth. The right question was "Has the baby dropped?" or "Is her heartbeat still sounding good?"—not "Can I swim in a meet next month for this insane German swim coach?"

So I didn't ask, and I didn't ask, and then finally, it was April 17, the date I was scheduled to be induced.

We'd scheduled the induction because I have that blood-clotting problem, Factor Five Leiden, and in order to keep it from damaging my pregnancy, every day I was pregnant I needed a shot of Lovenox, an anticlotting drug. Complicating the birthing process, my doctors told me that I needed to stop taking the Lovenox before I delivered if I wanted to have an epidural. (Apparently, taking the drug close to the time of the procedure is dangerous.) I wasn't sure yet if I wanted an epidural or not, but I wanted to have the option. Besides, planning the date suited me fine. I like to be prepared.

The day of the induction, David and I slept late (a real anomaly at our house). Then we swam, lifted weights, packed a bag, and in the early evening drove to the hospital. I won't get into all the details of Tessa's birth, but in a period of time you would probably consider wimpy, I asked for the epidural. Then, like a lot of my life, nothing momentous happened for a long time, and after that things moved really fast. Through the first evening and into the next day, nurses would come over, look at my progress, and say, "Hmmm, not much happening" or "Looks like this baby girl is going to take her time."

Then the midwife broke my water. *Boom!* Tessa was on her way.

Soon after, when my mother was stroking my hair, out of no-where, I snapped, "Get away from me!"

David and my mother, who birthed six children herself, turned to the nurses and said, almost at the same time, "I think she's ready to push."

As usual, they were right. I pushed four times (I guess all the core strengthening I'd done for years had paid off) and there she was.

Seeing Tessa was so amazing. I put her on my chest. She had my father's steady brown eyes, my mother's beauty, and she was really long. I'd worked harder for her than anything else in my life. David and I named her after a character in the movie *The Constant Gardener*. I don't care if she ever swims or ever wins a race. I just want her to be happy and to love whatever she's doing. I want her to experience the world as fully as she's able. Life can be hard sometimes. I want her to be strong.

The birth filled me with so much happiness. I had a child in my arms, at last. The years of infertility had been really difficult for me. I was used to being able to make my body do what I wanted it to do—for better or worse—and my inability to produce a baby had made me feel extremely out of control. A lesser source of joy, but a joy nonetheless: I was no longer pregnant. I'd been really ready to meet Tessa, ready to embark on being her mom. Plus, who am I kidding? I'm an athlete at heart. I wanted my body back.

About 15 minutes after her birth, Tessa latched on to nurse for the first time. When she finished, I handed her to David and looked down.

Let me say I know this isn't going to win me a lot of friends, so remind yourself right now, before you keep reading, that I'm like a stuntman or a contortionist or something. My work is my body. I've missed out on lots of fun stuff you did while I was counting tiles on the bottom of a pool. I definitely cannot write a legal brief or make a crème brûlée as well as you can.

My stomach was flat.

It wasn't hard, but it was flat. Somehow that reminded me of Michael's meet.

"Hey, Dr. Zafran," I asked as casually as I could before he left the room. "Thanks so much for everything. I've been meaning to ask you something. When can I start working out?"

I loved my doctor. He was hardworking, unpretentious, and a real jokester, just the kind of guy you want on your team. "Well," he said, "you can work out with weights tomorrow if you want, which I don't think you will, but don't do cardio for six weeks."

"Okay, thanks," I said, turning my attention back to Tessa.

At that moment, I didn't fully understand what birthing a baby does to a body. I didn't know that I wouldn't want to sit down, let alone work out on a leg-extension machine, for a while.

~ ~ ~ ~ ~

Becoming a mother changes everything, but it's also deeply grounding. It forces you to weed out distractions from your life. It compels you to define your values, to figure out who you are.

Mothering is also an entirely different way to relate to another human being from anything I'd ever experienced. By the time I had Tessa I'd been through two divorces: first from the sports producer Jeff Gowen, and then from an Israeli doctor, Itzhak Shasha, who'd helped take care of my father at the end of his life. I was more than a little wary of another marriage, but I was determined to be the best mother to this child that I possibly could.

I was not yet planning on training for a fifth Olympics, but I knew I'd be striving toward something in my life pretty soon—I always am. Being an athlete and a parent is its own particular challenge. You're not stuck at the office at all hours, but you're never completely free of the job. You're always thinking about how you're treating your body. You need to schedule your day around your training, and when you eat and sleep. I believed I could be an exceptional swimmer and an exceptional parent. I didn't think excelling at those two things simultaneously was too much to ask. But I knew I'd have to stop worrying about pretty much everything else. Most significantly, I had to rule out having another child until after the Olympics, at which point I wouldn't just be an old swimmer, I'd be an old mom.

I couldn't have asked for a better role model than my own mother. She was born in Los Angeles to a Hollywood family. Her father worked in the Paramount Pictures sound department, and in the 1940s, he won two Academy Awards. My mother had one brother, who died when she was only a year old. Perhaps to make up for the loneliness of losing him and being raised as an only child, she had a lot of kids herself—my two oldest brothers, Michael and Kirk, born in 1958 and 1960, during a brief first marriage. Then, in 1963, she married my father and had four more children with impressive speed: Rick in 1964; Brad in 1966; me in 1967; and my sister, Lara, in 1968. My father adopted Michael and Kirk, and they changed their last name to Torres. To this day my mother jokes that she had four boys and then a tomboy (me), so she had to keep bearing children until she got a girlie girl.

Even with such a big crew, and enough money for babysitters and housekeepers, she did everything for us herself. She packed our lunches, she hosted sleepovers, she lobbied to make sure we got the best teachers in our schools, she was president of the PTA, and she made sure we all behaved reasonably well. On top of that, she also drove us all over Los Angeles County to every kind of practice and game you can name, and not insignificantly, at least to the male coaches and teachers in our lives, she looked drop-dead gorgeous doing it. All the men we knew were constantly falling in love with her. I was extremely proud of this. My mother was trim, blond, proper, young, and mesmerizingly beautiful. Yet if someone messed with her kids—watch out!

Not only did my own mother teach me how to be a parent, she gave me my competitive streak and my athletic skill. Any sport any of us kids did, she did right alongside us. If we swam, she swam. If we skied, she skied. If we worked out in the weight room, she worked out in the weight room, too. Through that openness and enthusiasm she taught me that athletics can be a way to connect with people, that sports can be a means of staying alive to new experiences, and that the body can keep the heart and mind young. If I'd been into building model rockets, I'm sure she would have found a way to teach me about enthusiasm, connecting with people, and staying young through model rockets, too. But I was into sports, and so my mother taught me how to live well through sports.

Later, coaches and other athletes built on her lessons, further showing me that sports needn't only be about self-glory and winning, that athletics can make a positive difference in many areas of people's lives. But the idea that sports can inspire? I learned that first from my mom. My mother continues to inspire me through her strength, grit, grace, and beauty. She makes time for her six children, her twenty grandchildren, her husband, and herself. She still plays tennis every day. She still comes to all my important swim meets and she still always cries. She's lived her life extremely well. If people feel that I've inspired them, the credit belongs to her first.

My greatest hope is that I can pass along to Tessa what my mother taught me. Like me, Tessa's a pistol: energetic, intense, out-going, and strong-willed. Like me, she gets bored easily. Her favorite game is "race." She is going to need sports. Of course, I'd like to inspire people besides my daughter. I'd like to set an example for anybody who doesn't want to give up on themselves. But if I had to pick just one person to inspire, that person would be Tessa. So about a week and a half after delivering—once I could comfortably walk and sit again—I left Tessa with a sitter and started mothering by example. I took my postpartum body to the gym.

Michael, the German coach, had still been calling, asking me if I'd swim in his meet. I'd been saying, "No, I can't do cardio for six weeks. I really don't see how this is going to work." But then, while I was working out, doing some triceps extensions, something in the mirror caught my eye.

I thought to myself, *No way. It can't be. . . .*

Yup, sure enough, it was my obstetrician, Dr. Zafran.

I didn't call out to him, because I was worried that maybe he'd been kidding that day in the hospital, right after Tessa's birth. Maybe I wasn't supposed to be back in the weight room so soon.

But Dr. Zafran saw me and he walked over. There was nowhere to hide. "Hey, DT," he said, calling me by my initials, putting a hand on my shoulder. "I see you're working out."

My heart started racing. "I thought you said it was okay to be in here the next day."

"Yeah, that's fine," he said.

We made small talk for a few minutes, mostly about Tessa. Then I finally came out with it. "You know, the coach at the aquatic center wants me to swim in this Masters meet. It's like a week and a half away. I know it's totally crazy. But I feel pretty good. Is that okay?"

Dr. Zafran leaned back against a machine for a few minutes. You could almost see him thinking. "You know what?" he eventually said. "Go ahead and swim. You know us doctors, we always tell our patients six weeks, but we really have no idea."

He asked a few questions, such as if I was still bleeding a lot. I said no.

"Okay, DT," he said. "Just be careful."

Back at home, I called Michael and told him I would swim. The next day, I went to the pool.

~ ~ ~ ~ ~

At Coral Springs, when a rec—or recreational—swimmer walks into the complex, the front office gives that swimmer a little slip of paper to hand to the lifeguard. It's just a simple system to help keep track of who's there. Ten days after I gave birth to Tessa, Chris Jackson, the Masters coach, happened to be the guard on duty, blasting AC/DC, when I showed up at rec swim that first day.

I handed him my slip of paper. He didn't say congratulations or even hi.

"Excuse me—hello?" I prodded. By that point, we'd become friends.

Chris looked up and said, "Oh, my God." Last time he'd seen

me, just two weeks prior, I'd been more than 30 pounds heavier, with Tessa the watermelon sticking out front.

The week leading up to the meet I trained three times, about a mile per session, mostly with my training partner, Barbara. Then, on the day of the meet, the first Saturday in May, David, my mom, Tessa, and I all headed to the pool. It was too hot for Tessa to be out on the deck, so she stayed inside with my mother and I ducked in every 30 minutes to see if Tessa needed to nurse. The meet was short-course, meaning that all events were in the 25-yard pool. My goal was to swim 50 yards in 23 seconds—one second slower than my personal best time.

I was entered in two relays. My team won one and placed second in the other. I swam each of my 50-yard freestyle legs in 24 seconds, one second slower than I'd hoped. I know this would not be a big deal to a normal person—what's a second or two a couple weeks after having a baby? I should have felt blessed that I was out there at all. But I'm not normal about speed. I don't care about reasons or preexisting conditions. I just care about my time. However absurd a goal 23 seconds might have been, it was my goal. I had not met it. I was bummed.

After my race, as I was warming down dejectedly in the kiddie pool, Michael, the German coach, unruffled as ever, walked over and started talking. At that point, I was not telling myself, *I just had a baby, I should give myself a break*. I was screaming inside my head, *Why the hell am I going this slow?*

Meanwhile, Michael squatted nearby and in his German accent started giving me a mini lecture about amino acids. He'd worked with a bunch of older athletes before, he said, and taking an amino acid supplement made a big difference in their recovery times. As Michael later spelled out in detail, amino acids are the building blocks of proteins in the body, and proteins are the building blocks of muscles. So if your body needs assistance building or repairing muscle tissue, amino acid supplements can really help. Eventually, he even recommended a brand, Fitness Nutrition Amino Acids, that had been tested in a lab accredited by the World Anti-Doping Agency and found to be free of all banned substances. But I wasn't really integrating anything he said at that moment. He was acting as if I had a future in sport.

"I can't keep swimming," I said, interrupting him. "Didn't you see my time?"

One of the best things about Michael is his ability to put things in perspective. He's put my performance in perspective for me dozens, if not hundreds, of times.

"You have to realize what you just did," Michael said that day as I was still wet. "You have no core strength whatsoever. You can't just expect to have a baby and be so close to your best time."

~ ~ ~ ~ ~

I would love to tell you lots of stories from Tessa's first few weeks and months. But I can't. I was too exhausted from waking up three times a night. My memory was not functioning very well.

I do remember sleeping in the hospital on Tessa's second night in the world. At two in the morning, I heard some cries and started thinking, *Who the heck's baby is screaming that loud?* It was Tessa.

Tessa, right from birth, was hungry, very hungry, and she had a bloodcurdling scream. I breast-fed her, sometimes for 90 minutes at a stretch, and it never seemed to be enough. Nobody thought I was going to breast-feed, including my mother. It's true, I didn't love it, but I wanted to do what was best for my kid. Tessa wanted to eat, a lot, and my breasts grew very sore. She's never been even a tiny bit shy about letting me know her needs.

In the early weeks, I spent my days doing mom stuff—errands, changing diapers, baths, nursing, more diapers, more nursing, the standard drill. I'd go work out at the gym, but since I wasn't pregnant anymore and I'd finished swimming in Michael's meet, I was done in the pool (at least I assumed I was done in the pool—until I was pregnant with baby number two). But David hadn't been swimming just because I was pregnant. David had been swimming because it made him feel good. He didn't want to quit Masters. Just the opposite, in fact. He wanted to push himself to the next level.

One night, when we were crashed out on the couch, trading Tessa from knee to knee, David said, "You know, there's another meet in a couple of months out at Stanford, the Masters World Championships."

"Okay," I said, half awake.

"Well, I'm thinking about swimming in it. Will you swim with me?"

"Aaahhhh, I guess so," I said. "I just need to find someone to watch Tessa a few times a week while I train."

I didn't really process what I was saying. Then I fell asleep.

The strange part is, the first month or so postpartum is really good for swimming. Your tendons and ligaments are all still loose from all the pregnancy hormones, the same ones that help create enough wiggle room in your pelvis for you to push a baby out. The postpregnancy body also still has a lot of extra blood, which means extra oxygen and extra kick. So aside from the fact that you can't sleep at all, you're overwhelmed and distracted, your breasts ache, and you never get a moment of peace, it's a great time to be in the pool. So I rolled with it. I trained three days a week with Chris Jackson, or with my friend Barbara, for an hour at a stretch. I wasn't thinking about anybody's future at that point except

Tessa's. But Michael's talk about my postpartum performance had at least gotten through to me enough that I wasn't saying, "No way, I'll never swim."

So with three-and-a-half-month-old Tessa in tow (and a stroller, Pac N Play, diaper bag, breast pump, and car seat; ahhhh, the joys of motherhood), David and I flew out to San Francisco. As I've said, I love landing at that airport and driving south. The Sierra to the east, the Pacific to the west—nothing beats that view. It felt especially great to be there with a kid. Tessa, while exhausting, had given me new motivation. I liked how it felt to be wrapped up in this new phase of my life, to be at a swim meet as a mom.

More than 5,000 Masters swimmers had flown in for the event, and they brought the most incredible energy. Masters swimmers are amazing that way. Nobody's obligated to be there. Nobody's shown up just to please a parent or a coach. Every swimmer has carved out time from his or her busy adult life to train to compete. The feel is totally different from an age-group swim meet. Kids often have no idea how lucky they are, or what their parents have sacrificed to enable them to swim. But for Masters swimmers, just getting to a Masters meet takes money you've earned yourself, vacation days that you prize, and more self-discipline than most people will ever know. You have to get yourself up at five in the morning because you want to swim well. You need to dig down in yourself and find the strength within to get through long, tough sets.

I was planning on swimming two relays, plus the individual 50-meter freestyle. Like everybody else, I was there to have fun— no real expectations—but immediately after arriving I became incredibly nervous. Everywhere I went, people started walking up to me, telling me how my comeback (what comeback?) was part of their hopes and dreams.

"Oh my God, it would be so great to have a 40-something in the Olympic Games!"

"You have to do this for all the moms out there!"

"Go for it, Dara! Do it for us! You'll be the hero of the middle-aged!"

Hundreds of people must have approached me during that first day. I tried to put it all aside, to let them worry about themselves, and just focus on finding a place to breast-feed Tessa before my race. But all the expectations put me into overdrive. I wanted to swim the 50-meter freestyle in less than 26 seconds. (The race was long-course, which meant it would be much slower than the Mother's Day meet in Coral Springs, as you don't get speed off the turn.) But after the loudspeaker blared, "Four-time Olympian Dara Torres!" I just kind of freaked out. The attention overwhelmed me. I felt off balance on the blocks. Not as badly off as I had felt in the preliminaries of the relay in the 1984 Olympics, but from the dive I could tell I was trying too hard, spinning my wheels.

At the wall, I wound my turnover too fast. I touched in 26.4 seconds. I won, but once again, I was disappointed about my time.

So that was it, I figured: I was done with competitive swimming. I'd raced in two meets and it was confirmed: My body couldn't produce much speed anymore. But I still had a couple of relays to come, and quitting to me is even worse than losing, so I stuck it out. The next day, I was scheduled to swim the leadoff leg of a coed 4 × 50-meter freestyle relay with my old friend Rowdy Gaines. As always, before the race I was ridiculously nervous. But this time I decided to use my old tricks for calming myself down. I did my warm-up swim and put on my iPod. I pulled my energy inward. I tried to find my old groove.

About 20 minutes before the start, I nursed Tessa in the bathroom and passed her to David. I reminded myself: *I'm a mom first and a swimmer second. Whatever happens out there, the most important thing in my life has never even put her tiny little toes in a pool.* At the start, to prove to myself I was serious, I dried my block with a towel. Then I splashed my arms with water, listened for the whistles, and crouched for the starting signal.

This time, throughout the 50 meters, I felt loose and relaxed. When I touched, Rowdy had this huge grin on his face.

I smiled and shrugged as if to say, *At least that wasn't totally embarrassing.*

Rowdy kept smiling. He cocked his head and pointed up to the scoreboard.

I'd swum my split in 25.9 seconds, fast enough to have qualified for Olympic Trials.

5

~ ~ ~ ~ ~

On Losing My Father and Gaining a Coach

I never told my father I was swimming again. He died five
months after Tessa was born, and he was just so happy to see me
with a child that I couldn't bring myself to complicate his joy. I
know this will sound a little strange, but while my father was totally supportive of me, he was never that interested in my swimming. He didn't keep me out of the pool (except when I was a kid
and my grades were bad), but he wasn't much engaged with my
life in it, either. I accepted this. It never occurred to me not to accept it. I loved him, and he loved me, and when I saw him, unexpectedly, in the stands at the 2000 Olympic Trials with a "DARA"
hat on his head, it was one of the happiest moments of my life.

When I was a kid, growing up in Beverly Hills, my father wasn't
around all that much. My parents divorced when I was five, and
my father was a workaholic who spent most of his time in Las
Vegas. He managed or owned a series of hotels there, including
the Fremont and the Aladdin, in which Elvis and Priscilla Presley
got married on May 1, 1967, just a couple of weeks after my birth

on April 15. Later, my father bought the Thunderbird casino, which he turned into the El Rancho. He also ran the Riviera, where Dean Martin owned a stake and sang in the lounge. This was during the Rat Pack years. My father was very private and didn't tell me too much about his work life. But I do know he ran with a famous crowd and sometimes got mixed up in their dealings.

Shirley MacLaine used to tell a story about my dad. As it goes, one day Dean Martin returned earlier than expected to the Riviera, and when he arrived he found that my father had rented out his penthouse while he was away. In typical Las Vegas fashion, or so the story goes, Dean didn't get angry. He got even. Dean had his agent pay a bellboy to collect all my father's clothes and pile them on the floor in Dean's penthouse. Dean's agent lit the clothes on fire, then called the fire marshal on the way out the door to say he smelled smoke.

I loved my dad and was proud of him, but as a kid money and celebrities were not my thing. I was a tomboy, a serious tomboy. Even as a little kid at El Rodeo Elementary School in Beverly Hills, fancy Los Angeles culture didn't suit me all that well. I got in trouble a lot, mostly for fighting with boys. More than once I was suspended from school. I had no interest in dresses, dolls, hopscotch, or other stereotypically girly things. My main concerns were sports and winning. I wanted to get picked first for the team, any team, and I usually was.

Both my parents had nice big houses, but I didn't care much. Every possible waking moment I was playing tennis, or basketball, or soccer, or racing people on my bike. Both my parents also had pools, in which my mother taught us how to swim. My parents stayed very close after they divorced. I know it's unconventional, but even after my mother married Ed Kauder, my longtime stepfather, the original Torres family stayed tightly connected right up until the end. My mother would come with us kids when we spent our summers at my father's second house on Long Island, in Quogue. She'd stay for two weeks, leave to see her husband for one, then come back. Even separated, my parents continued raising us as a team. If any of us kids acted up, my mother would get my father on the phone. He was the disciplinarian, and he'd dispense the necessary scolding from Las Vegas if need be.

Life at my mother's house was always fairly laid back, but at my father's there were lots of rules: no feet on the furniture, no elbows on the table, no drinking water before you finish your soup, no T-shirts with stretched-out collars or cutoff jeans. Lunch was at noon, and you had better be there. If you sat on a couch or a decorative pillow, you had to fluff it back up again when you stood. And dating? Lord knows when my father thought dating would have been okay. I never even asked.

But those summers in Quogue were also full of freedom, and they laid down a bedrock layer of family love. My father's house was right across the street from the beach, and we spent most of our days there, except lunch. When my sister, Lara, and I were little we'd just play around in bikini bottoms; I was so rough-and-tumble I'd sometimes be mistaken for a boy. At low tide we'd climb down a ladder with buckets and dig for clams. Sometimes we'd swim across the bay for sailing lessons. Otherwise, we'd just mess around. When we grew older, my mother drove us 45 minutes at 4:30 or 5:00 in the morning to keep up our swim training because Quogue didn't have a pool. Every Sunday, the whole family had ribs and potato salad flown in from Noonan's in L.A., all of us reaching and bumping elbows to get our fill. My father didn't appreciate the poor manners, but he was proud of his scrappy brood. With so much competition at the table, we all had to learn to eat fast.

I love looking at pictures from those times—the six of us kids so healthy and tan, our skin spotted with salt. In one, my hair is all tangled and matted from the ocean, and my father's wearing a baseball cap backward, a sure sign that he was on vacation and very relaxed. My father and I look so happy together, almost giddily happy, like we have some kind of secret. His hand hangs around my shoulder. We both look blissfully casual and secure, like neither of us could ever imagine a day when he wouldn't be there to protect me.

When I was seven, my older brothers started swimming at the Beverly Hills Y, and I followed right behind. Before making the swim team you had to graduate from the "minnow" group to being a "shark." That didn't take me long—I was in a hurry, of course. But once on the team I found that I had to practice, when all I really wanted to do was race. One of the family's favorite stories from those early years is of the young me at a swim practice. At that point I was just a tanned, bony, hypercompetitive jumble of long feet, long hands, and long limbs. The coach had us doing a set of freestyle sprints. Thinking I was really slick, I swam halfway across the pool and then turned around in the middle and swam right back to make sure I'd beat my teammates to the wall.

I wasn't a great fit for the Beverly Hills Y. For a time I even quit swimming. Then an old teammate called to tell me that Terry Palma, a laid-back, even hippielike coach I'd swum with a few times at the Venice Swim Club, had moved over to train at the Tandem Swim Club of Culver City. Culver City was way less fussy than Beverly Hills. I gladly joined him there.

I was a good natural swimmer, though I hadn't yet developed a work ethic, either in the pool or anywhere else. My father more than occasionally grounded me from practice so that I could focus on my school work. But my will to win was overwhelming—so overwhelming that no matter how many practices I missed, I still won my races, much to the annoyance of my siblings and team-mates. Around age 12, under Terry's guidance, I started to apply myself a little. I began swimming six days a week, about 5,000 yards each time. In 1980, I set the national age group record in 50-yard freestyle for 11–12-year-old girls in the United States Amateur Athletic Union. It was my first real record, set at 24.66 seconds. The time was a testament to my competitive spirit, if not my dedication and discipline. I still have the gold-crested blue ribbon framed on my office wall.

Of my six brothers and sisters, I am most like my dad—at least that's what everybody always said. Like me, he cared deeply about his family. He knew how to work hard when he had to. He was very strong-willed. My father was Jewish, born to Spanish immigrants, but the only word of Spanish he ever spoke to me was *Paciencia!* Patience! Neither of us liked to wait. My father was also an old dad—I was born when he was 50 years old. He never cared about his age, or let others define him by it, and I guess we're alike in that way as well. When I was a teenager, he'd sometimes take me out to the movies with my friends. I remember once he asked for the senior citizen discount. I was mortified, but his age never bothered him in the least.

My father and I grew very close during the years I lived in New York. But by the time I moved back to New York, after training in California for the 2000 Olympic Games, my father, then 82, was spending a lot of time in Palm Beach, Florida. He'd tired of the cold winters, and most of my brothers were then working there in a real estate business my father had started for them. At first I just flew back and forth down the eastern seaboard, so I could see my father regularly. But in 2001, my father was diagnosed with colon cancer. For a time, I kept flying back and forth. Then, in 2002, I decided to move down to Florida and into my father's house.

Shortly after my father's diagnosis, he had a surgery to remove the diseased part of his colon. This left him with a colostomy bag, which he hated. But after his plumbing was reattached and the bag was gone, his pride was restored and he seemed to be okay. Then, a year after that colon surgery, a scan showed a spot on my father's liver. Now he needed another operation to remove the diseased part of that organ, plus he had to start on chemotherapy, and this made him increasingly sick. My mother, loyal to the end, got an apartment in Florida and drove him to all his doctor's appointments. By that point, I'd married again, to one of my father's doctors, an Israeli guy named Itzhak Shasha whom everybody called Ike. My father liked Ike. He was 19 years older than me, he was good to my father as a doctor, and he was Jewish, so my father didn't mind that Ike and I got to know each other when I'd visit my father in the hospital. I'd spend hours giving my dad manicures and pedicures and massaging his feet. Ike would come in and chat with my dad and eventually me, too.

From the beginning Ike and I had an easy, great rapport. We'd both been married before—Ike had been married twice. I converted to Judaism for him, and after our wedding, we tried to have a baby together. We even tried a couple of IVF cycles. Neither worked, which was extremely painful to me. By that point, each of my five siblings had three or more children. Why couldn't I have one? I wasn't so old—35, then 36. I was ovulating. I was in great physical shape. Nobody could find a reason why I couldn't conceive. The stress of infertility didn't destroy my marriage, but it certainly didn't help, either. We were married only 16 months, from July 2003 until December 2004.

After we split, Ike went back to his second wife, and I sublet a friend's condo near my father's house on the beach. I ran on the sand and swam in the ocean, and spent as much time with my father as I could. Sometimes he and I would just hang out. Other times we'd go out to lunch or dinner. Meals were a huge part of my father's life. He loved to cook, and when he couldn't cook anymore, he liked to take his family out to eat.

One of my father's greatest wishes was to see me have a child. "I've been waiting my whole life for this," he told me about a year before he died, when I told him I was pregnant with Tessa. I think he meant it, too. Seeing me with Tessa made my father ecstatic. And the two of them were so much alike. Tessa is strong-willed. She knows what she wants. She knows how to get it. She's a natural leader. She likes to be the boss. Tessa is also such a bright, smart kid. My dad was an extremely intelligent man. Tessa made my father very proud.

Before Tessa was born I'd moved from my condo on the beach to Parkland, where I still live, but I used to bring Tessa with me on the 45-minute drive up to Palm Beach to see my dad once or twice a week. My father wasn't well enough to play with her on the floor, and that really wasn't his style anyway, so I'd lay her down with him on the hospital bed he'd had installed in his house. The two of them, at opposite ends of life, found a simple game. Tessa would grab the belt of my father's robe. My father would make a show out of trying to yank it away. My father got such a kick out of Tessa, with her mischievous grin and her wide brown eyes. Tessa is so clearly a continuation of him. My father gave so much of himself to her. I still can feel him watching her every day.

As with so much else in my life, the end came slowly for my father, and then it came so fast. He'd had cancer for five years, but for almost all of it he'd managed to get around all right. At some point he needed a cane, then one week, in late summer of 2006, he deteriorated and needed a walker. A couple of weeks later he was in a wheelchair, and by September he couldn't get himself out of bed. About a month before he died, I could tell my father needed something to boost his spirits. I'd always tried to do that for him, so around noon one day I called and said, "Hey, I'll come up tonight and take you to Morton's Steakhouse." I knew how much my father loved going to restaurants. Morton's was one of his favorites.

That evening, I left Tessa with David and drove from my house up to the coast. With help, my father and I made it into my car. We even made it to Morton's. But soon after we arrived we both knew we'd overreached. My father needed help going to the bathroom. The host was extremely accommodating, but this was just a huge blow to my father's pride. He'd always been the big man, the caretaker, the guy who could handle anything. We tried to eat a few bites, then conceded. We asked for the check and retreated home.

"I really did that for you," my father told me once we'd made it back to his house and my brother, Rick, had come over to help me get my dad back into bed.

I held his hand. "I did that for you, too," I said.

That's when it hit me that I was losing my father. He never went out to eat again.

In late October, the weekend before he died, I went to visit my father, as I did three or four times a week. My mother, as was often the case, met David and me at the house. Despite their divorce 30 years earlier, my mother nursed my father to the end. That day, my father lay in bed watching his beloved Fox News. My mother and I started talking over it, apparently too loud.

"Can you two take it somewhere else?" my father grumbled.

Initially, I took this crankiness as a good sign. My father had been too tired to be animated in recent weeks. Maybe he was regaining some strength?

But the next day my father felt worse, and the day after that my mother called to say he'd slipped into a comalike state. I drove up to see him again and found him in bed, not moving at all, with his mouth slightly ajar. I stayed by his side for an hour or two, wanting to be near him.

"Do you think I should sleep over?" I asked my mom. I was nervous to leave, but knew I couldn't help.

"No, sweetie," my mom said, "you go on home to Tessa."

So I did. I went home and curled up with my baby. I even fell asleep in her room.

In the middle of that night, at about 2:30 A.M. on October 31, 2006, our phone rang. David came to wake me. My father had passed away.

I knew my father was dying, but it still was a shock. For a few minutes I thought, wrongheadedly, that I could fall back to sleep. But then I pulled on some clothes and drove back to my father's house. When I arrived, the paramedics were just zipping my father into a body bag. They paused and stepped away so I could say good-bye in private. My father's face in death looked exactly as it had the night before. His open mouth upset me. When I went to kiss him, he was cold.

For the next year I'd cry at the drop of a hat. I'd pass a restaurant my father liked, or glance at one of the pictures of him I had framed in my house, and dissolve into tears. In one of my favorite photos my father is walking down a sidewalk in New York with a package under one arm. He looks terrific and really dapper, in a suit with no tie, a white shirt buttoned to the collar, and a sweater vest with cables. At that moment in his life he was young, maybe in his late twenties, and he had a winner's smile. I was not even born yet. The sun is shining and my father's hair is brushed back, like I sometimes wear mine now.

~ ~ ~ ~ ~

My father died just as I was getting serious about swimming again, just as I was allowing myself to believe that I could compete as a 41-year-old mother in the 2008 Olympic Games. I can't say the swim training really helped with my grief. But I learned to work through it, and that helped me later on.

During that fall I'd finally found a working-mom-like swimming groove. Midmornings, a sitter would come for Tessa and I'd drive through Parkland to the Coral Springs pool to train with a 6'5" 28-year-old Bulgarian named Ray Antonov. Ray was just about the best training partner I could ever have hoped for. He'd swum the 100-meter freestyle in the 2004 Olympics in Athens, and his best times for 100 meters were generally about a second and a half faster than mine. To me this was motivating without being devastating. I have a lot easier time being beaten by guys. The way I see it, men are supposed to be faster than women. So it's okay if you lose to a guy, and if you win it's doubly great.

Besides, Ray had impeccable European manners and was unfailingly solicitous, always calling out when I was still swimming with my former training partner, Barbara, or the Masters team, "Dara, when are you going to come train with me?" Ray, it must be said, was also fantastic to look at. I know he'll blush like crazy if he ever reads this, but Ray is incredibly handsome. And it didn't hurt that he liked to kiss me four times on each cheek before we hopped in the pool.

During that first week or two after my father's death, I'd often hang my head over the pool gutter as my goggles filled with tears. Every day I hoped swimming might take my mind off my loss, but then I'd remember all over again that while swim races are distracting, swim practices aren't. It's just you and your thoughts there in the water, lap after lap after lap. For weeks I did my workouts with a knot in my stomach and little but my father's death on my mind.

Chris Jackson was still my primary coach. Three times a week he had me doing 4,000-meter practices, focusing on my aerobic base. Sometimes Michael Lohberg, the gruff older German, would come over for a couple of seconds and tell me that my kick was sputtering or my hands were crossing under my body when I pulled the water. But still, despite my growing impatience, Michael wasn't interested in me. He was focused on training a German breaststroker named Anne Poleska, and he led practice for a bunch of fast international swimmers in the Coral Springs pool in the afternoons after they got out of school. Most of the kids were living with host families so they could train with Michael, who had a great reputation abroad. I knew what these kids' lives were like. I, too, had lived with a host family when I was 16 and training for the 1984 Olympic Games. I would have liked to train with them, but Michael, contained and methodical German that he is, hadn't invited me yet.

I don't know if he was waiting to see how I was going to handle being a mother and an athlete, or if he was waiting for me to regain my focus after my father's death. But Thanksgiving came and went, Christmas came and went, and Michael still didn't want to coach me. Finally, in February 2007, Michael asked me if I would like to travel with him and the elite kids to a training camp in Saint Croix over spring break. It wasn't a permanent invitation to be coached by him. It was more like a tryout. I said yes.

At that point Tessa was 11 months old, so I wanted her to come to Saint Croix, too. Since Tessa was coming, I asked my mother and stepfather to join me, to watch Tessa while I practiced. (David needed to be home working.) That trip was my maiden experience of learning firsthand that 39 years old is a hell of a lot older than 15. The kids all gave me my own lane at practice, partly because I couldn't keep up with what they were doing, but I also think they were worried about kicking me. The kids also all stayed in crummy apartments, four or five to a room. I'd had a lot of roommates in my life. I wanted, and needed, a good night's sleep. My mother, stepfather, Tessa, and I stayed in a hotel.

In some ways I felt younger being around the kids, especially when we were all snorkeling or throwing a football on the beach. But in other ways their youth made me feel old. One day, after practice, we all took a catamaran over to Buck Island. The coaches didn't come, it was just us swimmers, and the guys were putting their arms around their girlfriends, getting a little rowdy, trying to push each other off the boat. Twenty or 25 years earlier I would have joined right along with them, doing the same. But now was I supposed to chaperone? I kept worrying someone might get hurt. Afternoons I'd put Tessa in a stroller and walk her over to the girls' apartments. Tessa would crawl around and the girls would get a kick out of her—that is, until they got distracted by playing video games or trimming their bangs, or whatever it is that teenage girls do.

But Michael was terrific. I like to watch people, and I noticed right away that Michael had a great way of connecting with all his swimmers, from me right down to the 13-year-old kids. Under his contained German affect, he was warm, approachable, flexible, and calm, even in the face of outrageous goals. I'd seen glimpses of these qualities when I was nine months pregnant and he tried to enlist me in his Mother's Day Masters meet. But now I saw them up close, day in and day out, as he walked up and down the pool deck. Michael teased his swimmers, helped them stretch out tight muscles on the deck. He made his swimmers feel taken care of and noticed, and he did it all with a style that helped keep the mood light and tension diffused.

I liked what I saw in Michael on that trip, and I think he liked what he saw in me, too. I knew how to work hard and I had good technique—two of the most crucial elements to succeeding in the pool.

In Coral Springs, when training with young Chris, I'd been having problems getting too exhausted and breaking down with muscle fatigue. Chris had great energy; at age 30, he was still fresh and gung-ho. But Michael was not just physically weathered. He was a seasoned coach with a physiology background. He'd come up through the German training system, where he'd earned a degree at the Deutsche Sporthochschule, or German Sports University. He didn't just go with his gut. He collected data. After each practice he'd prick me behind the ear, drawing a few drops of blood to test the level of lactic acid in my body. Michael is one of the world's experts at looking at athletes' lactate levels to determine how hard they should be working out. His skills enabled him to determine how intensely I could work yet still effectively recover for the next day. I felt somewhat insecure about swimming at my age; I didn't know what my body could do, or even the best way to figure it out. But Michael had seen a lot of bodies over the years. In Germany, he'd led his team, SSF Bonn, to five German National Championships. He'd trained athletes from all over the world to 62 national records.

"Chris is going to kill you," Michael joked with me after we'd returned to Florida, and I think that was his way of signaling he was willing to take me on as my coach. The mechanics of my stroke had stayed intact despite my recent pregnancy and my advanced age. Michael saw it as his job to figure out how to keep me healthy, motivated, and strong—to combine my technique with a training regimen that would enable me to get in top sprinting condition without breaking down. (Breaking down is the swimmer's term for having such acute muscle fatigue that you can't keep training at a high level.) His primary insight was that I needed to swim a whole lot less distance, only five 5,000-meter practices a week. That might sound like a lot to a noncompetitive swimmer, but to me it was shockingly little. Twenty-five thousand meters was close to what I swam in two days of double sessions in college. But Michael understood physiology. Less was what my body needed. He believed I could win this way.

Now, under Michael's direction, on weekday mornings I swam with Ray and the German breaststroker Anne Poleska, and on Saturdays we all swam with the Saint Croix kids. He had me doing only one quality workout a week (a quality workout is really high intensity, just at a swimmer's threshold of being able to complete it). Michael and I made a funny pair: He's thick, I'm lean. He's laid back, I'm intense. He's hairy, I'm not. He's quiet, I like to talk. But we believed in each other. Between the two of us, we'd been around pools for over 75 years. I could not have achieved what I did without him.

Throughout that first year after my father's death, I could feel my competitive instincts rising back up. Every day I felt my father with me in the pool. Though I never told him I was swimming again, I came to believe that he would have supported me in try-ing to make it to a fifth Olympics as the oldest female swimmer in the history of the Olympic Games. I believe he would have been proud of me as a mother and an athlete, that he would have ap-preciated the discipline I was putting into following my dream.

Near the one-year anniversary of my father's death, I flew to New Jersey, where my father had been born, to visit his grave. I hadn't been to the cemetery before. I didn't have directions to his specific site. Yet he wasn't hard to find.

One mausoleum stood out from all the rest. It was bigger and fancier than the others, with two beautiful doors in front and room for a family of 12 inside. My father had actually moved in a couple of his siblings. As I drove toward it, I started laughing. *Is that my dad's? Did my father really have to build the biggest one?*

Sure enough, that mausoleum was engraved "TORRES." I sat down inside and cried for nearly an hour, heaving enormous sobs that in the end helped me move on from my grief. I left exhausted yet more at peace, and more determined than ever to make the 2008 Olympic team.

That night, back in New York City, I called my mother and asked her about the mausoleum. She told me my father wanted his grave site to be bigger than Zuckerman's, the guy buried next door.

I laughed again and felt even closer to my dad. Turns out I didn't inherit my competitive streak from only my mom.

6

~ ~ ~ ~ ~

On Being an
Older Athlete

Not even David understood how scared I was at first. After I qualified for the Olympic Trials, I could not get the idea of a tenth Olympic medal out of my mind. But what if I trained and didn't make the team? What if I set big goals for myself and failed?

From the minute I'd pulled myself out of the water at that relay at the Masters World Championships in the Stanford pool, people had been coming up to me, assuming I'd train for the 2008 Olympic Games in Beijing. I was flattered, of course, but my mind was short-circuiting. I'd be 41 years old at the Games. What's more, Tessa was only three months old. I was still breast-feeding. She couldn't sit up.

"Aren't you going to go for it?" David chimed in as we unpacked in Sun Valley, where we'd flown directly from the Masters meet so Tessa could visit my mom. David had never seen me swim in an Olympics. The idea sounded great to him.

I just shrugged and said, "I guess so." I had so many conflicting desires and thoughts. Apart from two Masters meets, I hadn't swum competitively in six years. What if I wanted to have another child? What if I was riding some weird postpartum high? What if my time in that relay with Rowdy had been a fluke?

Deciding to train for an Olympic team, no matter the situation, requires tapping into your deepest reserves of dedication, courage, and sacrifice. Not only must you be willing to put your personal life on hold, you need to tolerate treating your body like a machine and also risk enormous disappointment—that's the hardest part for me. You have to say to yourself, and to the rest of the world, I have a dream: I want to make the Olympic team. Then there's no guarantee you will. Emotionally, you're so exposed.

Over the years, as I've matured as an athlete, I've learned to tolerate exhaustion and, if necessary, physical pain (though, as you all know, I'm no masochist about it—no natural childbirth for me). But I'm as terrified as ever about losing. I hate to fail, even more than I love to win. Plus, let's get real: whom was I kidding? My chances of going to Beijing as a 41-year-old mother had to be pretty slim. If I actually achieved my goal and won a medal, I'd be the oldest swimmer ever to medal in the history of the Olympic Games. If I was going to try, I needed to be prepared for defeat, and that was really hard for me to accept. I knew I'd be completely devastated if I tried to make the Olympic team and fell short.

In Sun Valley, David, my mother, and I spent a few days cooing over Tessa, watching movies, napping, chatting, working out, and drinking tea, but I could never fully relax. Was I going to grab the opportunity or let it slide? I'd lie awake in bed, or stand in the shower, wondering if I had the nerve. At moments I felt close to having the inner strength, but I never got quite there. So after flying back home to Florida, I decided to go visit a guy I know named Bernard. Bernard is a psychic, a medium. Consulting the spirit world is a bizarre way to make a decision, I don't deny that. But as an athlete you get used to combining a day-in-and-day-out commitment to rational behavior (that is to say, training) with taking leaps of faith—in coaches, in teammates, and in yourself. There are moments when you just have to find a way to believe, even if there's no logical basis for it. That's why we all have superstitions: tapping home plate three times before setting up to swing, for example, or wearing one low ankle sock and one high knee sock at the big basketball game.

I'd first met Bernard when I was struggling with infertility and desperate for somebody to tell me there was going to be a baby in my future. Bernard had told me I'd have a baby girl, and he'd been right. Since that time he'd helped me find courage and clarity when I needed them most. Some people talk to God when they need reassurance. Some people bury themselves in statistics. My first approach is always to exercise—it clears my head and calms me down 99 percent of the time. But when exercise fails, I talk to Bernard. Now I wanted him to tell me if it was safe to allow myself to dream about making a fifth Olympic team.

In case you're wondering, Bernard does not look very transcendent. He's a balding guy, probably around 60 years old, with light brown curly hair. His office is in the back of his modest coral-colored one-story bungalow about 25 minutes from my house. The rug and the walls in his office are blue. He has Asian art and a picture of an American Indian chief on his walls, and geodes and cards that read "Reverend Bernard McCue" on his wide desk. Bernard reads palms and tarot cards to tell clients about their futures, but what I like best are his billet readings. Billets are messages to the spirit world. While Bernard is out of the room, you write down on an index card the names of three dead people and three questions you'd like him to answer. Then you fold your card up so he can't read it. When Bernard returns, he folds the card a few more times without looking at it, places it against his forehead, and starts talking to the dead people whose names you've written down. He calls them by name. They help him answer the questions you've asked.

The first time Bernard did this I started looking for hidden cameras. He muttered the names of the dead people whose names I'd written down, and he answered my questions, all without unfolding the card to see what I'd penned. But I didn't find any hidden cameras, and I stopped worrying about how he worked his magic. I felt Bernard had something to offer me. He'd made me calmer and more confident about attaining my goals. I chose to believe.

Now, in his office, back from the Masters World Championships and Sun Valley, in September 2006, I wrote down on my index card the names of three dead people and "Am I going to make the 2008 Olympic swim team?" Then I folded the card up.

When Bernard returned, he creased the card a few more times and pressed it against his forehead. "What? What . . . oh, yeah . . . ," he started mumbling to himself. "I see dolphins . . . swimming. . . . You need to follow your heart. . . . I hear many accolades in 2007 and even more in 2008. . . . You're going to inspire a lot of people."

I'm sure he said a bunch of other stuff, but that was enough for me. I left thinking, *Cool. I'm going to go for this. I'm going to make the team.*

I don't mean to say that from then on I was cavalier about making the Olympics as a 41-year-old mom. Just the opposite. All Bernard had done was pump up my nerve. Next, I knew, I needed to assemble the very best support crew possible, and together with that crew I'd need to figure out some secrets about maintaining athletic performance later in life.

By that time I'd already had some experience being the kooky old lady who thought she could still swim. When I was 32 and in training for the 2000 Games, I was vying to be the oldest woman swimmer to compete in the Olympics for the United States. In Sydney, when I was 33 years old, I became the oldest swimmer to ever win an Olympic medal. Back then, just like now, I thought of my age as no more than a number, not a big deal. But other people were constantly insinuating that age *did* matter, that even at 33 I was too old to compete.

"Don't you feel terrible in the water?" people would ask. "You know, being so old and out of the water for so many years?"

Questions like that really bothered me until I realized they had very little to do with me. Our whole culture is so terrified of growing older, so sure that life goes to hell progressively once you pass age 25 or 30 or 35—whatever number people have stuck on their heads. But I came to see such negativity as a reflection of other people's fears about life, a window into the ways in which so many of us are limiting ourselves and selling ourselves short. I decided, back then, not to live that way. I chose not to let age stop me—not at 33 or 41—and people have had very strong reactions to that. Along the way to the 2008 Olympic Games, I encountered two camps of people: one composed of doubters who absolutely could not believe that a 41-year-old mother could be one of the fastest swimmers in the world and felt sure I must be doping; and another composed of optimists who thought I was a hero for proving that middle-aged athletes had been underrated, and thought my attempt wasn't at all far-fetched.

I am not the first—nor will I be the last—athlete to achieve something remarkable after being supposedly past her prime. Ted Williams hit .388 when he was 39. Karl Malone earned a triple double in the NBA when he was 40. Jeannie Longo won a French time trial championship in cycling at age 48. And did you see the 38-year-old Romanian mother, Constantina Tomescu-Dita, who won the Olympic marathon in Beijing on the same day I swam in the finals of the 50-meter freestyle? I had to watch it on TiVo, but her kick was amazing!

I didn't consult any scientists to see if my comeback plans were crazy. I suppose I didn't want to hear if they were. But later I learned that lifestyle, not genetics, is the primary reason older athletes tend to slow down, and that made a lot of sense to me. Most people, as they reach their thirties, place more priority on their jobs and families, as well they should. But as a result they downgrade their workout goals from achieving personal bests to staying in shape. This might be the right decision for many. This might even be the right decision for you. But if you still have athletic ambitions, if you still want to compete and win, there's no reason you have to give up. Your body can still perform if you put in the effort—if you still do that 10-mile run or that long, hard quality set. You just need to be smarter about your training and more time-efficient. But chances are, if you're an older athlete, you're smarter and more time-efficient anyway.

So how long can peak athletic performance last? According to the Cardiovascular Aging Research Laboratory at the University of Texas at Austin, both elite and non-elite runners and swimmers can maintain personal bests until age 35, after which point (for most people, and the *most* is important) performance declines in a gradual, linear fashion until about age 50 to 60 for runners, or 70 for swimmers. Deterioration is exponential from there. The Cardiovascular Aging Research Laboratory also found that swimmers experience more modest declines than runners, and that swim sprinters, like myself, experience the smallest declines of all.

My favorite study about sports and aging comes from a runner and economist at Yale University named Ray Fair. This guy crunched piles of statistics on aging and peak athletic performance and created what he calls the Fair Model. Basically, he created a table of coefficients that enables older athletes to take their personal best times and compute how long they should expect to take to complete that same event at a specific point later in life (assuming they've kept training at the same level). According to the Fair Model, a woman like me, who swam a personal best of 24.63 seconds in the 50-meter freestyle at or before age 35, should expect to clock 25.37 seconds at age 41. Being off by .71 seconds according to the model didn't bother me. I just took it as motivation to train harder and smarter. As this economist-runner Ray Fair wrote in a paper titled "How Fast Do Old Men Slow Down?": "I am struck by how small the deterioration rates are . . . It may be that societies have been too pessimistic about losses from aging for individuals who stay healthy and fit . . . But then again it may be that" these findings "are only of interest to old runners as they run ever more slowly into the sunset."

In training for the 2000 Games, I learned a few lessons about what I needed to do, as an older athlete (a young 33 at the time!), to keep swimming fast. The first was that I couldn't train like I did when I was in my twenties and not break down. I needed to do less, which was hard for me to accept at first. Admittedly, my coach, Richard Quick, the one who smelled of sunscreen, understood this when I first flew out to Stanford at age 32 to see if I could still compete. But I did not immediately catch on. In my mind, working hard and training hard meant swimming many, many thousands of meters nearly every day. So even though Richard wanted me to swim fewer meters than the other girls (all but three of whom were at least 10 years younger than me), I didn't always comply. I still believed in a direct relationship between pain—or at least yardage—and gain. I could not yet hold in my mind that my older body could be different but not worse.

For a while I managed to pull off training as long and hard as the rest of the team. Or, I should say, I managed to pull this off for the first few days of each week, and then by Friday I was an exhausted mess. One Friday, in late October 1999, several months into my training, I showed up to practice so tired and broken down that I could barely lift my arms out of the pool. There was no fooling anybody, no willing myself through it, no sense in trying to swim. Richard instructed me to get out of the water and to go get dressed.

"You need to rest, do you understand that?" he said once I was back on deck in my street clothes, always a huge embarrassment to a swimmer during practice.

I nodded.

"You actually need to rest. For real. I don't want you doing one thing this weekend. Not even one."

As he was talking to me, I felt scared and chastened, like a little kid. Since college I'd been throwing in an extra run or spin class on my days off, thinking it would make my body stronger, that that would help me win. I'd always been fitter than the competition. I got that way by working out longer and harder (sometimes compulsively, when I had an eating disorder). Now, apparently, those days were over.

Richard's mouth kept moving, but I stopped being able to focus. In some corner of my brain I understood what he was saying: I needed to go spend the weekend on the couch.

So I went home and spent the weekend forcing myself to sit—not exactly my forte. I kept thinking, *Is this really the best way to prepare for the Olympics? Could a short jog or a spin class really hurt?* But somehow I managed to follow Richard's directive, and on Monday, as he had predicted, I felt great—energized and fully recovered for the first time in months. That Monday I swam one of the best practices of my life, and the contrast forced me to recognize how exhausted I'd let myself become. I wasn't going to win races by pretending I still had the boundless energy of youth. I was going to swim fast by paying attention to my body and allowing myself to recover.

~ ~ ~ ~ ~

The second lesson I learned leading up to the 2000 Games was that older athletes need to be strong.

They say the fountain of youth is in the weight room, and Robert Weir, my rival Jenny Thompson's strength-training coach, had really set me up to drink from it. Working out in the Stanford gym I'd put on 20 pounds of muscle. I could eventually bench-press 205 pounds. My bulging biceps made me feel invincible—and as every athlete, old or young, can tell you, feeling invincible is half the battle.

But there are different kinds of strength, and in truth, from the moment I collected my courage to vie for the 2008 Olympics, I knew that I was going to need a different strength-training approach. It's hard to move in a muscle-bound body, and speed in the water comes from flow and technique more than from brute power. A perfect stroke looks effortless and smooth. The swimmer ripping up the pool with the biggest guns is often not the same one who reaches the wall first.

Shortly after I'd talked to Bernard and really thrown myself into dreaming about a fifth Olympics, I took my car in for an oil change. I'm sponsored by Toyota. They'd set me up with a Lexus, and that day I was just hanging out at the dealership with Tessa, waiting for my car, when the general manager came out to chat. He'd read that I was swimming again, probably in that Mother's Day article about the Masters meet, and he told me about another client of his, the strength-training coach for the Florida Panthers. He thought maybe this Panthers guy, Andy O'Brien, could help.

For me, that was another one of those moments like the one I had with my dad and the waiter in the Chinese restaurant, when a total stranger starts talking about the very thing that's on your mind. Just that week I'd been asking around in local gyms, looking for a new strength-training coach. I took Andy O'Brien's number. What could it hurt?

On the phone I told Andy about my career and what I'd done to train for the 2000 Games—the leg-press pyramids, incline dumbbell curls, and upright rows. I felt proud and sure he'd be impressed when I told him the amount I'd been lifting. Then we set a date for lunch. This was in the fall of 2006, before Michael Lohberg, the German coach who'd approached me when I was nine months pregnant, had decided I was worth his time to train. But I was working on my dream, formulating my grand plan. So I asked Michael, despite his skepticism, to join us at lunch, too. (I figured he had to relent in the future.) I also asked Chris Jackson to come, as I was presently training under him.

As I later learned, even before he met me, Andy had decided I needed a new strategy in the weight room. It had never occurred to me that he wouldn't be impressed by my 205-pound bench press. But he wasn't. In his mind, if I'd won a bunch of medals training in such a crude way I probably could win more medals, even eight years older, if my workout was more sophisticated.

We were an unlikely crew, all of us there in our booth: me, the postpartum mother; Michael, the German who wouldn't train me; Chris, who'd first met me when I had a watermelon in my belly; and Andy, who looked so baby-faced and clean-cut, my first question when he showed up was "How old are you?" (Yes, I know I'm not supposed to care about anybody's age, but Andy looked 25 and was only a few years older.) Yet once Andy started talking, any fear that his youth equated with inexperience quickly slipped away. Andy knew more about muscles and how they produce movement than anyone I'd ever met. He explained, in that simple, clear way of people who really know what they're talking about, that speed derives from highly coordinated movements and fluid timing, not heaving big stacks of weights in the gym. Weight training, he said, grew out of bodybuilding, and while bodybuilding is great if your goal is to show off your physique, it's pretty counter-productive for a sprinter, as weight training produces a body composed of big muscles that have been trained to produce force individually, and usually only in a single plane of motion. Bodies like this are not balanced and coordinated. They waste a lot of energy just trying to move.

Even before our lunch arrived, I knew I wanted to work with Andy. I'd seen plenty of muscle-bound gym rats. I'm sure you've seen plenty, too. They move horribly, not fluidly, and I knew I needed to move fluidly in order to zip past those kids in the Olympic pool and take full advantage of my experience and technique. Even before our food arrived, I had a strong intuition that Andy could provide me with the right plan.

While still at the restaurant, Andy outlined what he had in mind. First he would watch me work out in the gym, taking careful inventory of my current strengths and weaknesses, looking at how I was using my strong muscles to compensate for my weak ones. Next he'd analyze my motions in the pool. Finally he'd come up with a specific training regime, which he'd change every five weeks. Andy, bless his optimistic heart, had already looked at a calendar and noticed that the swimming Trials for the 2008 Olympic Games were five weeks before the Games themselves. He wanted to put me on a five-week training cycle so that I'd be able to peak at both events. I loved his hopefulness and his philosophy. He wanted to train not just my muscles but my central nervous system, by which he meant my reflexes and coordination. His primary goal was to keep my body spry and fresh. This would also enable me to recover more quickly between workouts.

I was jumping out of my seat with excitement, ready to sign on. Michael, meanwhile, buried his face in the plate of crab cakes he'd ordered for lunch. Andy was not proposing the traditional weight-training regimen for a swimmer. (That was closer to what I'd been doing with Robert Weir in 2000.) So now not only was I far too old to swim, I wanted to use a flaky trainer. Michael was not impressed.

But I had a good feeling, and Michael wasn't my coach yet anyway, so I hired Andy. He watched me work out in the gym and watched me swim. Then he gave me some bad news: My body had recovered fully from my pregnancy with Tessa, but I was seriously out of balance. All the muscles in my body that pulled forward and down were very strong (from swimming for so many years). Everything that pulled back and up was weak. As a result I hunched, which I knew and disliked. I also moved inefficiently. No matter what made sense ergonomically, I'd contort my body into a position so that my strong forward-pulling muscles could do the work. In other words, I compensated for my weaknesses with bad form. If I wanted to reach my potential as an athlete, I really needed to stop.

To rehabilitate me (Andy actually used that word), he had me doing all kinds of crazy drills. I'd kneel on a balance ball with five-pound weights in each hand. I'd lie on a balance ball, weights in hand again, pretending to write letters in the air. I worked out the tiny muscles between my shoulder blades—muscles I never even knew existed. Andy's first goal was to straighten me out, to get me more mechanically efficient. I loved the sound of this. Despite the ways in which I'd been compensating, I always tried to be a stickler for technique. In fact, one of the keys to my success as an athlete is that coaches have always told me I have something like the kinesthetic equivalent of perfect pitch. I'm very good at mimicking motions that others show me how to do. I'm also able to execute movements repeatedly without losing my form.

So I started training with Andy in the Coral Springs Aquatic Complex gym. Andy couldn't always be there, as he had obligations to the hockey players on the Florida Panthers, but because I cared about form as much as he did, he felt confident I'd do my exercises correctly. All those tiny muscles in my back were very sore at first. But I believed wholeheartedly in Andy's plan. I can't say the same was true for the coach who wouldn't coach me, Michael. Every once in a while, he'd would walk into the gym while I was working out.

"Is that all you're lifting?" he'd say, seeing me on a Swiss ball making letters with five-pound weights.

I'd say, "Yup."

He'd get a disgusted look on his face and wander off.

I did feel kind of silly at times. But I'd decided I believed in Andy, and once I choose to believe in a person, I try to stop questioning and submit. It's funny, because in most parts of my life I do not submit at all. I can be really controlling in my household. Don't even try to tell me how to organize my refrigerator or hang my clothes. But once I sign on with a coach or a trainer, I choose to believe everything. I assume that person's approach is right (at least 99 percent of the time). I've seen plenty of younger athletes start second-guessing their training regimens after a tough practice or meet. I understand the desire to blame something or someone, but I believe it's much better to choose your program wisely in the beginning and then stay the course.

I actually think this is one of my greatest strengths as an older athlete: I'm very stable. I don't get skittish or do things halfway. Within a few months of working with Andy I was 12 pounds lighter than I had been at the 2000 Olympic Games, and I felt more lithe and stronger than ever. I didn't yet know how this would translate into speed. Andy had never trained a swimmer; I'd taken a big gamble on him. But I felt fantastic, and I really enjoyed what I was doing. I also had a safety net. Olympic Trials were still over 18 months away. I told myself that if I wasn't swimming fast by Nationals, in the summer of 2007, I'd stop working on those tiny muscles between my shoulder blades and go back to a more traditional strength-training approach.

~ ~ ~ ~ ~

The third lesson I learned about being an older athlete from the 2000 Games is that I needed to stretch.

By stretch I don't just mean bend down and touch your toes. By stretch I mean build true flexibility. It's a difference that, before those Games, I knew little about.

Picture it this way: Your hamstring is a rubber band. To touch your toes, that rubber band just needs to get long. If that rubber band gets long, then in some sense you've stretched, but that stretching alone doesn't do you very much good. If you want to do something dynamic, like walk or sprint, that rubber band needs to be able to stretch out and then snap back in. It's not just a muscle's ability to stretch out but its ability to lengthen and contract again that produces power and speed.

All swimmers know that stretching is important. If you start a stretching program and you gain an inch on every freestyle stroke, you'll gain about two feet for every 50 meters. Flexible muscles also let a swimmer generate more force through a greater range of motion, and that means more power through all parts of your stroke. Flexible ankles, for instance, allow your feet to act like flippers, leading to a strong kick. Flexibility also lets you move just the part of your body that you're trying to move; in other words, it enables good form. Just imagine a really stiff muscle-bound guy trying to swim. He may have an impressive physique, but because his body is rigid, his technique is lousy and he creates a lot of turbulence. Despite his strength, he can't swim fast.

I'd always known flexibility was important to a swimmer, but I'd never thought about how true flexibility really works until one afternoon, about two and a half months before Trials for the 2000 Games, when I drove over to a Pilates studio in Palo Alto, California. At that point my coach Richard, who was training me on the sly in Santa Clara, really believed in Pilates. He was still training my archrival Jenny Thompson at Stanford, so he had Jenny working with the head of the Pilates studio, and to diffuse the tension between us, he had me working with the studio director's open-minded assistant. One day, while I was on the Reformer—a piece of Pilates equipment—I noticed three other people in the studio, two guys in white T-shirts who were doing some strange kind of tandem bodywork on a client. The T-shirt guys were guiding the client's limbs into very specific positions. They'd push against the client's muscles and tell the client to resist. I had no idea what they were doing.

"What's that over there?" I asked my teacher. I'm sure I was staring.

"That's what you really need," she said.

"What?" I said. What I really meant was "No way am I doing that."

"Really," she continued. "That's what you need. When we're done here, you should go talk to those guys."

So after my Pilates session I approached them about their technique. I learned it was called resistance stretching and it was totally different from any other stretching regime I'd seen. These stretchers were using their bodies like weight-training machines. They'd move a client's limbs along a very precise path. Then they'd tell him to push back against that stretch. Apparently, it was a way to build strength and flexibility at the same time.

I have to say, I wasn't eager to try it. It looked too weird. But I knew, as an older athlete, I needed to be open to new ways of sustaining my body. I asked for the stretchers' phone numbers and I called the more senior of the two, Bob Cooley, the next day.

Bob, I can now tell you, is one of the most intense people I've ever met. The day I called him, he told me an incredible story. In 1976, he'd been in a horrible accident. He and a friend had been walking on Commonwealth Avenue, in Boston, when they'd been struck by a car traveling 40 miles an hour. Bob's friend was killed immediately. Bob landed in the intersection with a dislocated shoulder, the muscles of which contracted so forcefully on impact that they'd ripped apart his left humerus. He also got a concussion and sustained injuries throughout his body, and he spent the next year visiting physical therapists, massage therapists, orthopedic and neuromuscular therapists, and sports medicine practitioners, anyone who could help him move. Bob found that once his acute injuries had healed, old-fashioned stretching helped him the most. Yet it didn't help as much as he hoped.

So Bob decided to take responsibility for his own rehabilitation.

He knew he cared about his predicament far more than anybody else, and he decided to sit on the floor of his house, for an hour each day, until he figured out a stretching system that helped him move better. He'd once heard about a guy who'd decided to sit in a chair until he came up with a plan to make a million dollars. That guy wound up inventing a canister for reviving old dead tennis balls and saw his dream realized. Bob figured that if he gave it enough time and thought, he'd succeed, too.

Day after day, Bob sat with his legs spread wide apart, trying to lower his chest to the floor. Nothing happened for some time. Then one day Bob felt his chest lowering—and not just a little. Bob's flexibility seemed to improve all at once. That day Bob discovered, counterintuitively, that if he contracted his leg muscles at the same time he was trying to stretch them, they loosened up dramatically. He spent the next year and a half building a resistance-stretching regime around this central insight. Over time he settled on a series of sixteen types of stretches, each based on simultaneously contracting and stretching a particular muscle group.

If you've ever done yoga, this should make a tiny bit of sense. In yoga, you press your feet down into the floor at the same time as you reach your arms overhead. You make your muscles work in opposition. As a result, you build strength and you stretch.

I didn't really know what to make of Bob or his story, but I liked his conviction, so I told him I wanted to give it a try. To me, open-mindedness is crucial to athletic achievement. You can't keep winning if you're in a rut. If you stagnate, you lose. You have to keep your body fresh. But before Bob would stretch me, he insisted on stretching my coach, Richard Quick. So Richard and I met Bob at the Pilates studio. Bob pushed and pulled Richard every which way.

Richard loved it.

I was next.

It's really hard to describe what resistance stretching feels like. It's sort of like doing a yoga class where the teacher physically places you into lots of unusual poses. It's sort of like getting a massage where you have to push back against the masseuse, applying half the force. Bob manipulated my knees, thighs, arms, shoulders, back, ankles, hands, and core. At one point I was facedown, knees tucked under me in fetal position, with my hands grabbing a belt behind my back. Bob pressed my elbows up toward the ceiling and then pressed them back down toward the floor. Each time he applied pressure, he told me to resist. I was bent and rotated just about every way my body could move. It was not elegant or glamorous. I drove home telling myself, "Okay, that was really strange. But let's just see what happens tomorrow in the pool."

The next morning in the water I felt incredible—full of energy, riding high, like I'd been tapering for a big end-of-season meet. My shoulders were rotating in all directions without a hitch, which they hadn't done since I was in college, when I'd partially torn my labrum, the cuff of cartilage in your shoulder joint that holds the top of your arm bone. I still don't understand why resistance stretching works so well. Bob claims that his stretches follow traditional Chinese medicine meridians, or lines in the body that carry energy, so perhaps there's some benefit from an alternative-medicine standpoint. All I can say is what happened. I started working with Bob and his partner, Tom Longo, for an hour at a time, several times a week. Sometimes we'd meet at the Pilates studio. Sometimes I'd drive up to Bob's house in the Santa Cruz Mountains. Sometimes he'd come to the pool. He claimed his stretching would help me emotionally and psychologically, that it would help me overcome the mental obstacles that had been making it hard for me to win. As always with Bob, it was hard to parse his stories. But just as I felt with Bernard, I felt willing to embrace just about any idea that gave me confidence.

Five weeks after I started working with Bob—less than a year into my comeback and a month and a half before Olympic Trials—I entered the Santa Clara Invitational swim meet. Bob stretched me for 15 minutes on the deck right before each of my races.

In the 50-meter freestyle, I swam a personal best, 24.73 seconds, breaking the American record.

I was sold.

I started calling Bob my secret weapon. He and his partner, Tom, traveled with me to the 2000 Games in Sydney and stretched me before each race. I know I would not have won five medals without them. But before the Games started I'd had a falling-out with Bob over my swimming technique. Bob believed I should be swimming with my head out of the water so I would see where I was going. One day, not too long before we all left for Sydney, he'd even brought a video into Richard's office, making his case that a swimmer is like a motorboat. The bow should be up, out of the water, to take best advantage of the speed produced by the motor in the rear. Richard, good-natured as always, heard Bob out. He even paid Bob the respect of timing me in the pool with my head up and my head down (despite having explained to Bob that his theory was inherently flawed. A swimmer's motor is not just in back; a swimmer has motors, if you really want to call them that, all over the body, in the arms, legs, shoulders, hips, and core).

Needless to say, when Richard timed me, I swam faster with my head down. I swam that way in the 2000 Olympic Games. Bob, mad genius that he is, never fully accepted this. When I decided I wanted to train for the 2008 Olympics, I knew I wanted to work with a resistance stretcher, but I also knew it wouldn't be Bob.

~ ~ ~ ~ ~

That turned out to be one of those moments when hardship breeds opportunity, when necessity drives luck. I'd met Steve Sierra, one of Bob's disciples, a few years earlier. Steve was a former body-builder and gym owner who'd learned resistance stretching and become a professional stretcher himself, mostly working with professional basketball players, like Alan Houston of the New York Knicks. At that point Steve lived in Connecticut, a minor obstacle. But I wasn't afraid of calling people out of the blue. I'd once cold-called Colin Hay, the lead singer for Men at Work. So I found Steve's number and dialed him up.

"Hey, Steve," I said. "I have a proposition for you. What would you say to moving down here to Florida and stretching me as I train for the 2008 Olympic Games?"

This was more than a little random. As far as Steve knew, I was retired. He knew how old I'd be in Beijing. But Steve agreed to fly down to Florida and stretch me for a couple of weeks. The only hitch was that he now worked with a business partner, Anne Tierney. So she flew down to Florida, too. They stayed at my house, in our guest bedroom, and we all set into figuring out if we could function as a team.

Our routine was a little rocky at first, as we worked out the details of where I should get stretched, what time I should get stretched, how long I should be stretched for, what sequence of movements we should do, which stretcher should stretch which parts of my body, and how hard I should resist. Steve, poor guy, also had to figure out a way to deal with the fact that from the get-go Anne and I talked and cracked jokes pretty much nonstop, and when we weren't cracking jokes we were text-messaging each other. Steve is quiet, but Anne's a strong girl with a strong person-ality, just like me. We were either going to love each other or hate each other. We loved each other. In Anne I found one of my closest friends.

We also all found an easy groove together. After practice, around noon, three times a week, I'd come back to my house and lie on my living room floor with one of Tessa's pink flower bolsters under my knees. Anne and Steve would begin by mashing, or massaging me with their feet. Usually, Anne would sit on a chair near my head, working the sides of her feet into my arms and shoulders (an easier position from which to gossip), and Steve would sit in a chair at my side, working the sides of his feet into my legs and glutes (slightly quieter over there). They'd do this for 45 minutes, kneading lactic acid and small bits of scar tissue out of my muscles and the fascia that surrounds them. Muscle fibers, as we all know, loosen up fairly readily, but the fascia around muscles is denser and far more difficult to break down. So Anne and Steve mashed with their feet. Using their leg muscles, they didn't tire as quickly and they could apply more force.

After the mashing, Anne and Steve started into the resistance-stretching sequence proper, over 90 minutes of pushing and pulling at my limbs as we worked through sets of opposing muscle groups. The point was to rejuvenate my body from the inside out, coaxing all my muscles through their whole range of motion—lengthening all the way out, then shortening all the way back in. The sequence seemed really complicated at first, but in time it became second nature, like a dance routine. For one stretch I'd roll onto my stomach and tuck one leg underneath my chest, in what yogis call pigeon pose. Anne would then lean her torso against my extended back leg, forcing my heel in toward my butt. In other exercises, Anne and Steve would manipulate me at the same time. For instance, they'd work together on my tensor fascia lata, a muscle that starts on the outside of the hip and extends down the leg. I'd lie on my back and Steve would use his hands and shoulders to externally rotate my thigh. Meanwhile, Anne would stand at my feet, pulling inward on my calf.

At this point, in the early winter of 2007, I was completely invested in making the 2008 team but I had yet to race in anything other than a Masters event. FINA, the international governing body of swimming, requires a swimmer to sit out for a nine-month period from events they recognize (this does not include Masters) after declaring an intent to come back and swim. So through that winter and spring I was just biding my time, not racing in big meets, building my team. Once Anne and Steve moved down to Florida, I felt everything was in place. Michael was coaching me, I loved my workouts with Andy, and the stretching made me feel younger and looser than I had in years. Some women my age use the word "maintenance" to refer to face-lifts and Botox injections. Maintenance, for me, was resistance stretching. As Steve used to explain to people who'd see him stretching me and stare, an athlete's body is like a race car. You don't get a race car to go faster by doing more laps around a track. You get a race car to go faster by improving its mechanics, by making certain each piston is firing perfectly, by ensuring every component is oiled and working its best. The same is true for a body. Biomechanics are everything. Overworking gets you nowhere.

That spring, I turned 40 and Tessa turned one. We had a little party in the park for Tessa, and I stuck to my routine. Weekday mornings I'd swim with Ray, Anne Poleska, and the Coral Springs Swim Club National team, and on Saturdays I'd swim with the kids from Saint Croix. I swam five workouts a week, as opposed to nine in college, and I loved the rhythm of my days—swim, gym, stretch, and then play with T. Every day I made a point of doing something to aid my recovery. Some days I'd visit a chiropractor who worked his bald head into a frothy sweat as he buried his hand under my shoulder blade. On other days I'd book a massage.

I found one of my two masseuses, Jonathan, by asking David if I could use a gift certificate for a massage that had been sitting on his desk for months. Ten minutes into my first massage I was asking him, "Are you free for 90 minutes, two times a week, for the next two years?" The pressure felt perfect, as Jonathan has this amazing ability to get into my muscles and work out all my tension without making me grip the table in pain or leaving me sore the next day. Once a week, I also got a massage from a woman named Selina. Like Anne, she was young, fun, talented, and I had a ball talking to her.

I know being older is supposed to be a negative for an athlete, but I'm not blowing sunshine: I actually felt better than I ever had before. Sure, some days I was exhausted. Some days I had no faith and wanted to quit. But I understood my body better than I had in my youth, and I had the good luck and experience required to assemble such an amazing team. I was not making my comeback alone. I felt like a lead singer fronting a talented band. Tessa also gave me so much joy. Mori, her nanny, would arrive each morning at 7:30 A.M. For the next seven hours I'd train and recover. Then, at 2:30 P.M., when Tessa woke up from her nap, Mori would leave and I'd return to being Mom.

Lots of days, in the afternoons, Tessa and I would drive back to the pool to watch the kids swim. It's amazing how age builds appreciation. I now felt so happy to be near the water, still part of the swimming life. I loved the sound of other people swimming. I loved the kids' silly teenage humor. Some evenings I'd even invite a few over to my house to eat lasagna. Occasionally, my maternal instincts would take over and I'd offer to cut their hair.

Through that winter and spring, I was happier than I'd ever been, being an athlete, an adult, and a parent all at the same time. Tessa didn't care how well I swam. Michael didn't care how well I swam. No one cared how well I swam.

Except me.

In June of 2007, my FINA waiting period would be over. I'd signed up to race in the Sette Colli in Rome. This would officially signal to the swimming world that I was back.

Nobody had any expectations for a 40-year-old mother, but I was going to be devastated if I didn't swim fast.

7

~~~~~

On Competition

When I first arrived at the Sette Colli in Rome, I could not remember how I'd done it: How had I won so many races in years past? Most people think of swimming, especially sprinting, as a sport without much strategy. But there is more to winning a swim sprint than meets the eye (especially if you're used to watching swimming on TV). In fact, very little about competitive swimming meets the eye at all. Everybody can see who touches first in a meet, but only fellow swimmers understand what it takes to get there.

Winning a swim race, for me, depends on a million small things clicking into place in the span of 24 or 54 seconds (depending on whether I'm racing 50 or 100 meters). By the time you step on the block, you're either prepared to win or you're not prepared to win. One million things are far too many to think through in that short a time.

In the summer of 2007, it had been seven years since I'd competed internationally, and it was just one year until Olympic Trials.

If I was to succeed and make the Olympic team, I needed both to rediscover myself as a competitor and to reinvent myself. I'd been good as a kid, and even good at age 33 in 2000. But now I was in my forties. I'd borne a child. My body was different.

My first meet, in June 2007 at the Sette Colli, or Seven Hills, in Rome, kicked off the Mare Nostrum tour, a roving European swim meet that began in Italy, moved to Spain, and then ended in Monte Carlo a week later. The whole city of Rome, at once so old and so new, felt like the perfect place for me to reemerge. The pool there was beautiful, too, set up like a coliseum, the arena descending down from a tree-lined street.

We arrived a few days early to get over jet lag. By that point, the Coral Springs Swim Club was quite a crew. Our entourage included our German coach, Michael Lohberg, and some of the Saint Croix kids; my stretchers and me (Tessa stayed home with David; I didn't think putting her through the flight plus the time change would do either of us much good); Ray Antonov and Anne Poleska, who'd both competed in the 2004 Olympics; plus a growing collection of international and college swimmers who'd been trickling in after they'd finished their exams. Anybody who was serious about trying to make the 2008 Olympics was now buckling down for a year to try. Among the college-age swimmers on our team were: Leila Vaziri, a backstroke sprinter who'd set a world record in the 50-meter backstroke; Julie Stupp, a breaststroker from Auburn University, where she trained with my old sunscreen-smelling coach, Richard Quick; Sharntelle McLean, from Trinidad, who also swam the 50-meter freestyle; and Leo Andara, a Venezuelan who swam the breaststroke and individual medley. They were all exquisitely in touch with their bodies. They'd all been competing year-round for years.

One of the most important skills for a competitive swimmer is the ability to dole out energy in very precise doses. To win in the finals of a race at a big meet like the Olympic Trials, Olympic Games, or World Championships, you have to burn up enough speed in the preliminaries to make it to the semifinals, and enough speed in the semifinals to make the finals, but all the while conserving juice. (Other, smaller races only have preliminaries and finals.) Energy consumption is not something you can think too much about in the moment. You cannot set the dial on your internal motor to 95 or 98 percent. So for a novice, or someone who's been out of the pool for a long time, winning a swim meet can be tricky. Along with the countless other things that you might blow—getting off the blocks quickly; keeping a tight, streamlined position on your dive and turn; timing your finish to avoid gliding or half-strokes; keeping your head down on the touch—you can't win if you don't make it to the finals, but you also can't win if you arrive at those finals too spent to swim fast when it counts.

One of my biggest goals for Rome and Monte Carlo, and for my other competitions that summer, was to start establishing my prerace routine so that everything would be automatic and seamless by the time I reached Beijing. No detail was too small to obsess over or want to get just right. In the past, before each race, I'd warmed up twice. I would swim about 1,000 meters 90 minutes before my heat. Then I'd get out, hang around and get a massage, and then get back in, finishing up another 200 or 300 meters about 30 minutes before my heat. Now that routine struck me as too much hopping in and out of the pool. I wanted to warm up once, about an hour before my start. Then I'd stay on dry land while Anne and Steve stretched me out and I put on my racing suit and mentally prepared.

Whether I warmed up once or twice might seem unimportant. And maybe it is. But I believe you have to decide that all the details matter. If you don't, you'll let 1 or 2 slip, or 10 or 50 or 1,000 slip, and then you won't be the fastest swimmer anymore. When I was training for the 1984 Olympics at Mission Viejo, a sociologist named Daniel Chambliss watched us at practice nearly every day. Chambliss then wrote a book called *Champions: The Making of Olympic Swimmers.* That book totally captures the details-matter mind-set. I know it's a weird thing to say, but swimming is sort of like one of those Impressionist paintings made with millions of dots. Sure, a dot is a dot. What's the big deal? But if you care enough to make each dot the exact right size and the exact right color in the exact right place, something amazing occurs.

Chambliss understood what so many people miss: Swimming fast is not just about having big hands, or big feet, or flexible ankles, or a high percentage of fast-twitch muscle fibers, though all those things do help. Swimming fast is about having the mental discipline to get every last detail right, every single day. "The champion athlete does not simply do more of the same drills and sets as the other swimmers; he or she also does things *better,*" Chambliss wrote. "If you swim sloppily 364 days a year, nothing great is going to happen on the day of that one big meet, no matter how excited you get. . . . These little things matter not so much because of their physical impact but because psychologically they separate the champion from everyone else. Having done the little things, the champion can say, 'I have done what no one else has done, and I know it; and they know it, too.' The truth is simple: Most swimmers choose every day not to do the little things. They choose, in effect, not to win. . . . In some sense, everyone 'could' win in the Olympic Games, but 'could' doesn't count. The gold medal is reserved for those who do."

That captures my philosophy pretty well. I try to do all the things other swimmers don't. I believe it's the reason I've gotten faster as I've matured. I fine-tune everything—my training, my racing technique, my diet, even when I sleep. I make sure the people around me are positive and good for my mental state. I watch what I put into my body—no coffee, no alcohol. I drink my Living Fuel shake for breakfast (it's a combination of freeze-dried berries, protein extracted from brown rice, herbs, minerals, vitamins, and healthy bacteria) and take 10 tablespoons of amino acids a day. When people accused me of doping, I, like Michael Phelps and a handful of other top athletes, went straight to the United States Anti-Doping Agency and asked to be tested to the fullest extent of their abilities in order to clear my name and relieve my stress. I want to be direct about this: I don't dope. I never have and I never will. As soon as I came back at age 32, the allegations started flying from people too cynical and closed-minded to believe a middle-aged person can still be competitive in sports. But my detractors don't understand how much I put into my swimming performance. I've sought out the very best trainers, body workers, and nutrition. I'm 100-percent committed to executing perfectly every detail that might help improve my performance. I'm committed every day.

In Rome, one of my goals was to start fine-tuning my relationship with Michael, who as I'd predicted had relented and let me join his team. We'd never traveled together to a meet as swimmer and coach, and, to be honest, we were out of sync. On our second day there, after a morning workout, Michael and I went to a trattoria for lunch. I'd felt good in the water physically, but emotionally I felt exposed. This was the first time I'd ventured out into the world as that 40-year-old former Olympian who thought she could still compete.

I needed reassurance and I fished for it—always a big mistake.

"Do you think I can still do this? Do you think I can still swim fast?" I asked Michael over our pasta.

He sat across the table from me like a papa bear, warm, authoritative, and a little distracted. "I think you can do well in the 50, but I'm not sure how well you'll do in the 100," he replied in his matter-of-fact German way.

Then he went back to his lunch.

I know I can sometimes seem tough and confident on the surface, but really I have two opposing sides to myself: the fierce competitor who thinks she can swim faster than anybody else, and the vulnerable woman desperate to please others and afraid to fail. That day at lunch I felt vulnerable. I didn't say anything at that moment, but Michael's comment stung. In my own head I was already winning, not only in the 50-meter freestyle in Rome but in the 100-meter freestyle, too, and in 50s and 100s in dozens of other meets in other countries across the globe. Part of training, for me, is believing I'm going to win. I need to imagine victory—that's how my mind works. Once I actually win or lose a race, I register that information. I'm happy if I win and I'm unhappy if I lose, but it doesn't change my mind. I keep wanting to win, and I keep imagining that I'll be able to do that. No win has ever been satisfying enough to keep me from wanting to race again. No loss has ever been so devastating that I've hung up my goggles for good.

Mark Schubert, the coach who trained me at Mission Viejo when I was only 16 years old, helped shape my competitive psychology. He believed that with enough hard work I could always win. As a young coach in his early twenties, Mark decided the way to be a really great coach was to tell his swimmers they were great, then hold them accountable for being that good. He'd stand on the pool deck, above his athletes in the water, and scream down at them as he paced along the lanes, "You can win this race!" or "You can make Nationals!" or "You can set a world record!"—

Me, as a baby, in 1967, with my brothers Rick and Kirk in our house in Beverly Hills. We're all still very close. Back then I was too young to be competitive!

THE AMERICAN NATIONAL RED CROSS

This certifies that

DARA TORRES

is qualified as a
SWIMMER
having passed the required tests at
BEVERLY HILLS YMCA

6-21-74

Date Course Completed

R. M. Oswald
National Director
Safety Programs

My Red Cross card, which I earned at age seven for being able to do 100 yards, breaststroke; 100 yards, sidestroke; 100 yards, crawl; 50 yards, back crawl; turns (on front, back, and side); a surface dive; disrobe, float with clothes for five minutes; a long shallow dive; a running front dive; and a 10-minute swim.

This is one of the two days my father went to the beach in the more than 30 years he owned his house in Quogue, on Long Island. Here, he came with us when we took our boat to a little island off the inlet to have a picnic with a few other families. I'm six years old.

Preparing to race in 1976 (hence, the swimsuit). No cap, no goggles, and I'm not seeded first, as I'm swimming in lane two.

Every day in Quogue my dad sent Rick, Brad, Lara, and me out to the beach. By 1978 my two oldest brothers, Kirk and Michael, were 18 and 20 years old, and didn't always come.

Me with Colin Hay, lead singer of my favorite band, Men at Work, in 1983. I missed practice to track him down at his hotel in Hollywood. I'd bribed him to get this picture with a scrapbook I'd made of Men at Work clippings from *Tiger Beat* magazine.

Rowdy Gaines and me at Olympic Trials in 1984. I still had a huge crush on Rowdy.

Mark Schubert coaching me at Mission Viejo, leading up to the 1984 Olympics.

Coach Richard Quick training me at the Stanford University pool in 2000 when none of the other girls were around.

My father, Ed Torres, and my daughter, Tessa, five days after Tessa was born in April 2006.

My beautiful mother and me and Tessa, who is cranky after getting her four-month vaccines.

David, Tessa, and me in Sun Valley, Idaho, Christmas 2007. I didn't ski that year because I didn't want to risk getting hurt and interrupting my Olympic training schedule.

At home in my kitchen with Tessa a few weeks before Olympic Trials, in June 2008. I put this picture on my iPod and looked at it constantly when I was away from Tessa during my Olympic training camps and at the 2008 Olympic Games in Beijing.

Almost my whole family, at Olympic Trials in Omaha, Nebraska, July 2008. My brother Brad and seven of my nieces and nephews are missing.

My stretchers, Steve Sierra and Anne Tierney, stretching my hamstring at the Shangri-La Hotel in Singapore, a week before the start of the 2008 Olympic Games.

My friend and stretcher, Anne, and I separately got pedicures in Singapore. Back at the hotel, we compared. Her toes say, "GO DT." Mine are painted with American flags.

My start in the 4 x 100-meter freestyle relay. I'm swimming the anchor leg. Natalie Coughlin, sitting on the side of the pool next to the block, swam the lead-off leg for us.

Waving to my stretchers, Anne and Steve, during the medal ceremony for the 4 x 100-meter freestyle relay. I'd be coming home with at least one silver medal. I was so happy and relieved.

My friend Jack Renaud surprised me with this cake at Golden Goggles, an annual awards ceremony for swimmers, in New York in November 2008. I blushed like crazy when the waiters set the cake on the table, but I was very touched.

Reunited with my coach, Michael Lohberg, Florida, after I'd returned from the Olympics in Beijing and he'd finished his treatment at the National Institutes of Health.

whatever giant step he believed was at the very far end of their grasp. A lot of people thought he was crazy, but his methodology worked. Mark had more swimmers win races, more swimmers reach Nationals, and more swimmers break world records than just about anybody else around. He did it by first pumping up his swimmers' confidence. Then he taught them what they needed to reach their goals.

In Rome, the day after the trattoria lunch, I motioned Michael over to my lane during workout. "You know, Michael, I'd just really appreciate it if you didn't say anything negative to me before I swim."

He looked at me sort of blankly. "What are you talking about?"

"You know, that comment you made yesterday at lunch? That you didn't think I could swim well in the 100? You make these little comments, and they really upset me, so I'd really appreciate it if you'd stop."

I wasn't out to challenge Michael's authority. I believed in his workouts and I followed them to a T. I just can't tolerate negativity from my coach before a race. If another swimmer or an outsider wants to talk smack about my racing ability, I can deal with that. (I even find that motivating sometimes, like when my modeling agent, Dieter Esch, didn't think I'd be able to make the 2000 Olympic team.) But part of a coach's job is to set a swimmer's expectations. I didn't want Michael's expectations to be low. Nearly everyone in swimming has his or her own psychological tricks. I later came to realize that Michael was just protecting himself, claiming he had no expectations of his swimmer so those expectations couldn't be dashed. Rowdy Gaines used to prep for races by composing the speeches he was going to give after he lost, apologizing for his dismal performance and declaring his retirement from the sport. Personally, my mentality is to aim high. I cannot tell you how many hours I've spent in practices imagining that I'm winning races. The way I'm built inside, I can't see wanting to swim in a race at all if I think I'm going to lose.

Even before I swam in Rome, I could feel my own expectations start to surge. My initial plan for this comeback had been to focus on training for the 100-meter freestyle so I could make it onto the 4 × 100-meter freestyle relay, the lowest bar for a swimmer like me to get onto the Olympic team. (The top six finishers in the 100-meter freestyle make the team, as opposed to only two in most other events.) But now, in my head, I was making the team in the 50-meter freestyle and in the individual 100-meter freestyle, too. That would put me in four events in Beijing: the 50-meter freestyle, the 100-meter freestyle, the 4 × 100-meter freestyle relay, and the 4 × 100-meter medley relay. If you finish in the top two in the 100-meter freestyle, you also earn spots on the 4 × 100-meter freestyle relay and the 4 × 100-meter medley relay. So then I started worrying—prematurely—about whether my body could withstand that much swimming: If I made all those events, or so I daydreamed, I'd probably need to drop the individual 100-meter freestyle. But maybe I wouldn't. Could I still win the 50-meter freestyle if I swam the 100-meter freestyle, too?

The day of the 50-meter freestyle in Rome, I swam in the preliminaries, qualified for the finals, warmed down for a few minutes, threw on an oversized T-shirt and a pair of sweatpants, and walked over to the diving tower for Anne and Steve to stretch me out. I was just where I needed to be, or so I thought. My time was 25-low ("low" is swimmer slang for a time ending between .01 and .5 seconds; "high" is for a time ending between .5 and .99). More important, I was confident that my age wasn't so obvious in the water. I felt like a swimmer like everybody else.

But as Anne and Steve stretched me on the diving tower, Michael walked by and laughed. Not just a little bit. He belly laughed, like he couldn't keep it in.

"What?" I asked him, wondering what was so funny.

"WHAT ON EARTH ARE YOU DOING?" he yelled.

"This is my stretching," I said.

He just walked away, shaking his head.

This was not what I wanted or needed from my coach, as you can probably guess. Then, as I was contemplating whether I should talk to Michael again and tell him that this, too, was counterproductive for my psychology, a British swim coach approached.

"My swimmer was in your heat," he said to me in his cockney accent.

"That's great," I said. I didn't know what he was getting at, but I assumed he must have walked over to say something nice.

"She came out of the pool and she said, 'That Dara Torres in my heat, she's older than my mum!'"

The British coach thought this was pretty funny. I can't say I agreed.

As I've said, for me, winning races takes more than just developing a good plan and then sticking with that plan even when it gets painful and boring (though it certainly takes that). It takes building and protecting my confidence, so at the starting signal I feel fully prepared and relaxed. The mental part is really important to me. I spent a lot of years swimming inconsistently due to my youth or my eating disorder, or both. So that day, in Rome, I put back on my iPod to protect my mental space for the rest of my stretching session.

Later that day, I placed second in the 50-meter freestyle, touching in 24.93 seconds, swimming only three tenths off my American record of 24.63 seconds. I won the 100-meter freestyle, swimming in 54.63 seconds, only two tenths off my personal best.

Seeing me compete seemed to change something in Michael. After the meet ended, I heard him telling the rest of his swimmers, "You guys should really do some stretching."

He never doubted me again.

~ ~ ~ ~ ~

Being competitive is like being thirsty. You can satisfy the need temporarily, but that doesn't mean it stays dormant for long.

I've been a competitor my whole life. I've raced in swim meets since I was seven. I've also competed, every day, with whoever happened to be at my side. This, I've been told, can be tiring. As a kid, I competed with my siblings in just about everything under the sun—Ping-Pong, foosball, pinball, skiing, who could finish dinner first. As an adult, I still compete with my loved ones, much to their annoyance and chagrin.

For instance, one of my best friends, Tommie Nichols, won't play golf with me anymore. "I love her to death," she once told a reporter who'd called to find out what I was really like. "But oh my gosh, don't ever go out on a golf course with her. I've been playing golf since college, and she just took up the sport, and she's immediately hitting these 300-yard drives. It's pretty hard on us hackers. She never starts at the women's tee. She refuses to do that. So do yourself a favor: Don't play golf with her, okay?"

I compete with Tessa's father, David, too, and he has let his views on this be known. One night when we were out to dinner I overheard him telling a friend, "When we go on bike rides, she's gone."

"That's not true, D," I said across the table. (I call David and Tessa "D" and "T," and they call me "DT.") "I wait for you."

David didn't say anything. He didn't have to. He just raised his eyebrows, resting his case.

In the lead-up to the 2008 Olympics, I wanted to be careful

not to overly indulge all my competitive energy, as I had when I'd first started training for the 2000 Games. So I was happy to be training in the relative backwater of Coral Springs, Florida, close to family and friends and far from the hothouse of U.S. swimming that is California. Except for 1988, when I was a college student, I had never trained for an Olympic Games without uprooting my life. It felt great to be staying in my own house, hanging out with my nieces and nephews up in Palm Beach on weekends, and sleeping in my own bed. Tessa did not choose to be born to a mom who was training for the Olympics. She needed a calm, stable, loving mother. And I needed the calm, stable love that came with being her parent, too.

Our afternoons and evenings together kept me centered. Yes, I had big goals. Yes, I wanted to win at the 2008 Games in Beijing more than I'd ever wanted to win in an Olympics before. Yes, I wanted to prove that having a fortieth birthday is no reason to give up on your physical gifts. But I was a mother first and an athlete second. My daughter—not winning—was the most important thing in my life.

Practices with Michael were not swim meets. I swam only five times a week, about 5,000 meters per practice. Our team worked hard together, but we kept it light. If possible, I'd try to arrive first, at 7:40 A.M. for an 8:00 A.M. practice, because even when it comes to something as seemingly minor as getting to practice, I prefer to win. But once there I was not locked in conflict, as I had been with Jenny Thompson during our months together at Stanford. Before diving in, my handsome Bulgarian training partner, Ray Antonov, would kiss me four times on each cheek. Michael would pass out our printed workout sheets, I'd place my water bottle in the shade under my starting block, and then I'd get to work. My goal in the water was to perform each set Michael requested to his exact specifications. I'd give him grief sometimes, teasing him about needing to get a workout or take a vacation. He'd poke back, calling me "the queen" or "diva," making fun of my age and entourage. But when he asked for twelve 25s on 40 seconds, I did twelve 25s on 40 seconds. When he asked for six 50s of backstroke on 50 seconds, I did six 50s of backstroke on 50 seconds. Each morning I plastered my workout sheet against the end of my lane with pool water. That enabled me to double-check his instructions each time a new set began.

I also saw it as part of my job to keep practice fun. Positive energy doesn't just appear each day. You have to generate it. This is a responsibility shared by everybody on a team. "Hey, Sharnty," I'd call out to Sharntelle, the Trinidadian sprinter who happened to be a really sexy girl about 20 years younger than I. "I heard you had a fun weekend!"

She'd blush, and maybe we'd hear some good stories. Other days the swimmers would rib me.

"Hey, DT," someone would yell, "I heard you were going up for *Dancing with the Stars.*"

"No way!" I'd say. "I can't dance!"

No one ever tried to argue with that.

The truth is I was just so happy to be there swimming. If you've ever let go of something you'd loved but taken for granted, and then fought to get it back again, you'll know what I'm talking about here. These were bonus laps I was swimming. I felt really blessed to be at the pool, even when practice was tough. One day, about an hour into a quality workout—one of those once-or-twice-a-week just-barely-possible sessions designed to break you down and build strength—Michael called all of us to the center of the pool for a much-loathed drill, vertical kicking. For vertical kicking you have to hoist your torso out of the water, using only a flutter or dolphin kick. On that day we had to do it for 40 seconds, 12 times, on intervals of a minute and 15 seconds. (This is harder than it sounds.) For the last 10 seconds of each vertical kick we also had to be in "streamline" position, meaning that while still kicking we had to extend our arms straight overhead, one hand on top of the other, just as we would if we were going to dive or come out of a turn off the wall. (This is a lot harder than it sounds.)

"This sucks," I yelled after the first vertical kick, trying to distract my teammates and myself with some good-natured griping. The banter took us about halfway through the drill, at which point we were all too exhausted and miserable even to complain. Eventually, Michael even stopped calling out times, as everybody's eyes were on one of the three or four large clocks posted around the pool. We all knew exactly when we needed to pop up to our vertical kicks, when we needed to streamline, and when we could finally sink back down. Despite the lactic acid burn in my legs, I made a point of doing every hundredth of every second of every vertical kick. Swimmers know full well that every second has a beginning, a middle, and an end. So I rose to my kick in time for the first hundredth of each second, and I made a point of staying up, streamlined, until the last hundredth of the last second at the end.

The fall and winter of 2007 and 2008 were filled with practices and meets, with the occasional surgery thrown in. In November 2007, I flew to Germany for a meet and broke the American records in the 100-meter freestyle short-course and the 50-meter freestyle short-course (admittedly a kind of esoteric race, but it made me feel good). While there, my shoulder didn't feel right. Both Michael and I worried that I wouldn't be able to maintain the intense practice schedule required over the next seven months to prepare for the Olympic Games. So while still in Germany I called my orthopedic surgeon, Joseph Chalal, and the day after I returned home, I had what he called "arthroscopic subacromial decompression," meaning he surgically went into my shoulder, shaved off some bone spurs, and cleaned up a partially torn rotator cuff.

For six weeks after the shoulder surgery I did a lot of kicking drills. Unfortunately, this exacerbated a knee problem I'd first developed in college, when I'd torn a ligament running stadium stairs. I had surgery again in early January 2008 to repair a tear in my meniscus. One of the hardest parts of still swimming in your forties is that by that point in your life you've done an awful lot of strokes (even if you've spent 14 years retired) and spent an awful lot of time in the weight room, too. Things break down, and if you want to keep competing, you need to get them fixed. You can't win any other way.

By the time I went into the hospital for my knee surgery, I didn't just want to make the 2008 U.S. Olympic swim team. I wanted to—and thought I could—make the team in both the individual 50-meter freestyle and the 100-meter freestyle. This would put me in four events, including the freestyle and medley relays, both of which were pretty much guaranteed medals, as few countries besides the United States have deep enough swimming programs to stock their relay teams with four really fast girls. The U.S. women have medaled in the 4 × 100-meter medley relay in every Olympics since 1960, with the exception of 1980, which the U.S. team boycotted. The U.S. women have medaled in the 4 × 100-meter freestyle relay in every Olympics since 1920, excepting 1980 as well.

As I practiced in that big, unassuming Coral Springs pool, Michael, while not making gentle fun, would help me break apart all the elements I'd need to perfect my swimming technique and win. He felt my body was hanging sloppily on my start, so I worked on keeping everything tight and straight, shooting like an arrow when I hit the water. On my turns he wanted me to bring my head down earlier on my roll. Off the walls we focused on getting good tension off the surface, not doing too many kicks, and starting into my stroke immediately. On my finishes he wanted me to rotate my shoulder, right at the end of the race, so I would have a longer reach. He also wanted me to kick right up to the wall, until my fingers had touched.

Stroke for stroke, on the surface of the pool, I'm as fast as anybody in the world. It's my ancillaries that need work. Michael left my breathing, my catch, and my pull alone. But all the stuff around it we fine-tuned. The goal was to make a perfect race second nature, so I could put everything together without thinking at the starting signal.

Not all swim meets are in Rome and Monte Carlo, let me tell you that. Most are in places like Omaha and Indianapolis, and in February 2008, Michael took some of his swimmers, including me, to Columbia, Missouri, for the Missouri Grand Prix. Given that this was February in Missouri, it was sort of raining and sort of snowing, and half of us got sick. But there we were. With only six months until Beijing, everyone with Olympic ambitions wanted to see where they were in their training—or to be more precise, everybody wanted to see if their training was producing race results.

The Grand Prix was set up to mimic the upcoming Olympic Games. The preliminaries of each event were held in the evenings; the finals were in the mornings, the reverse of how it usually works. NBC had negotiated this schedule so that the Olympic swimming finals could be aired live during prime time on the East Coast of the United States. That was great for NBC but not very popular with the swimmers, especially late riser Michael Phelps. Everybody is stiffer in the morning than at night. Everybody also has a lower core body temperature (due to the fact that you have less food in your system and you haven't been moving). All of this slows a swimmer down. So there was a lot of chatter on the pool deck about what combination of wake-up swims, hot showers, and caffeine everyone was doing, and what was working best.

More than a thousand swimmers showed up for that Grand Prix, mostly kids who wanted to test their skills against a fast crowd. Some of the younger swimmers had backpacks with stuffed animals hanging off the zippers, which I found kind of jarring— clearly, they were much closer to Tessa's age than mine. I carried my gear to and from the pool in my roller bag. I was trying to conserve my energy and not tweak my muscles. I didn't even walk too much. I did see some swimmers I knew from previous Olympics, but most were on the pool deck wearing intentionally silly sport coats doing video commentary for swimnetwork.com. Mel Stewart, who won two gold medals and one bronze in 1992, came over to give me a hug but then stopped himself short, patting the air around my shoulders instead.

"I don't want to mess anything up," he said.

I laughed.

He shrugged and went back to his video work, saying, "Hey, we'd all be in there if we could be winning."

I didn't race very often while preparing for Olympic Trials, but I'd signed up to come to this meet because I wanted to see where I was in my training and how much I'd recovered from my shoulder and knee surgeries. I entered only the 50-meter freestyle, because I didn't think my shoulder could handle the 100-meter distance only three months after my surgery. Anne and Steve resistance-stretched me for 20 minutes before and after each race. I warmed up only once, an hour before my start, as I had in Rome. When not in the pool I wore a knit cap, long parka, and Ugg boots, to keep my body warm. And as always, just before my races, I got completely nauseous with anxiety.

The Missouri Grand Prix happened to be the first time Speedo-sponsored athletes got to race in their new high-tech LZR racing suits. The suits were amazing feats of engineering, built out of fabrics designed to compress and streamline the body and reduce drag. But they were also so tight, and so temperamental, that changing into one was an arduous affair. To put one on, you first have to gather up one leg of the suit, like a pair of stockings. Then you slip in your foot, which is much harder than it sounds, as the foot hole is designed to be very tight so the ankle cuff doesn't ride up your leg. Once both feet are through, the next job is to pull the seat of the racing suit up to your own butt. If you don't get this right the first time, you need to start over. The material of the suits has almost no give. You can't reach down, gather fabric, and pull up farther on your hip, as you might with a pair of tights. Some swimmers resorted to putting plastic bags over their feet before putting on their suits so they could get their feet through the leg holes. I eventually decided to wear a man's suit instead of a woman's. I felt it fit me better.

That day I planned to wear a size 27 long, but the box with that size had been lost in the mail, so the Speedo representatives suggested I squeeze myself into a 26 regular instead. I ripped three LZR racing suits, each worth $500, leading up to my race. After the zipper on the third suit failed, with just 15 minutes until my start, I asked, probably too gruffly, the nurse in the first-aid station if I could borrow her room for a few minutes. Anne, my stretcher and invaluable companion, cut off the LZR racer. I put on an old blue racing suit I'd thrown in my roller bag just in case.

For the final of the 50-meter freestyle, I stood behind the blocks with seven other girls, all between 12 and 20 years younger than me.

I'd come truly to believe my own mantra, that age is just a number, so I was thinking about my race, not the wide gulf in our years, when the announcer called my name and the Mizzou Aquatic Center erupted in deafening applause. At first I assumed that Michael Phelps must have just done something. He was over in the warm-up pool and always pulling off something amazing. Then I looked up to wave and saw all the parents of the other swimmers standing and cheering. Their kids were their kids, but I was their age. That noise was for me. I was their swimmer, too.

I dried off my block with a towel, as I always do, lest I slip. Then I bent down in a track start, with one leg back, the other leg forward, toes curled over the block. Rowdy Gaines and I both began doing this kind of start back in the 1980s. Before that, all swimmers started with the toes of both feet curled over the end of the blocks. I was wearing an old pair of bug-eyed goggles, ones in which my childhood coach, Terry Palma, had duct-taped the sides in the early 1980s so I wouldn't try to look at the swimmers in the other lanes.

So here I was, racing again: same goggles, a generation later.

I waited for the starting signal, then I swam my heart out down the pool, touching the wall in 24.85 seconds, just ahead of all-star Natalie Coughlin and behind a 22-year-old named Kara Lynn Joyce.

Within minutes, Kara, Natalie, and I were all up on a small podium. A college student hung a silver medal around my neck.

"Can I see it?" a high school swimmer asked me after I stepped down.

I tried to be a good sport, but I hate coming in second. "Sure. You can have it," I said.

8

~ ~ ~ ~ ~

On Being a
Younger Athlete

In some ways, being a really young swimmer is a lot like being a really old swimmer. No one expects a whole hell of a lot from you.

In my prime I was constantly worried: Who's in the next lane? Am I racing against a world record holder? Will I swim up to other people's expectations? I spent pretty much all of my peak swimming years—then thought to be the late teens and early twenties—feeling like I wasn't swimming fast enough, like I was letting my coaches and my teammates down. But when you're a really young athlete or a really old athlete, no one assumes you'll win. I liked being Dara Torres, that unknown hyper kid from Los Angeles who could really sprint. I also liked being Dara Torres, that 40-year-old mom unexpectedly back in the pool. But when I was in my supposed prime, I never felt totally comfortable. I felt like I couldn't swim fast enough. How could I have? You can't swim a personal best every day.

In the summer of 2007, the U.S. Swimming National Championships were held in the Indiana University Natatorium, in Indianapolis. I must have swum in the pool two dozen times. My mother came to the meet, as always, and when we arrived she said, "I can't believe I'm at another swim meet." I couldn't really believe she was there, either. I was 40 years old. My mother had 20 grandchildren. She'd fulfilled her duty as a supportive swim parent at least a hundred times over. But there I was, swimming again, so there my mother was, supporting her daughter. At Nationals, in Indianapolis, the only people *not* surprised to see me were the natatorium officials, who were waiting to interview me when I walked through the door. The university was collecting oral histories for the pool's twenty-fifth anniversary. Guess who swam in the facility's very first event, in 1982?

At the time the Indianapolis pool opened, it was state-of-the-art. Some pools really are faster than others, and a pool's ability to reduce turbulence is why. Pretty much everything in swimming comes down to controlling turbulence. A swimmer can reduce turbulence by achieving ideal body position (particularly head position) through the entire stroke cycle, which can be difficult given how much movement is involved. Pools reduce turbulence by dampening waves. In basic terms, the deeper the pool, the faster it is. Six to eight feet is considered sufficient to prevent waves from bouncing off the bottom and interfering with the swimmers on the surface. But Indiana had built its pool to be nine feet at the ends and ten feet in the center, so it was especially fast.

Gutters make a big difference, too. They need to be right at water level and have deep pockets so they can suck in the waves and keep the wave energy trapped, instead of reflecting that energy back out toward the swimmers in the center of the pool. Even lane lines can be designed to mute water movement and thus increase speed. And once a pool gets a reputation for being fast, a mental factor kicks in. Swimmers think they'll swim fast in it, and that pretty much guarantees they will.

As I looked around the Indianapolis natatorium, I noticed that my name was up on the wall in three different places. Trials for the U.S. Olympic teams had been held there in 1984, 1992, and 2000, and the university had posted the rosters of the swimmers who'd made those teams. More embarrassing, a poster of my face hung down from the rafters. "Oh my gosh, there I am," I said to my mom, pointing up. I did feel honored, of course, but also mortified. What active athlete wants to be hanging from the rafters? It looked like they'd tried to retire my number, but since that's impossible for a swimmer, they'd settled for my face.

In non-Olympic years, Nationals is the biggest swim meet in the country. That year, they were great (apart from the fact that David and Tessa stayed in a different room so I could really rest; I felt guilty about that). I won the 50-meter freestyle in 24.53 seconds, setting a new American record. I also won the 100-meter freestyle in 54.45 seconds, and I stood up on the podium with Tessa in my arms and finally believed that it was possible that my fastest swimming was really still to come. Now that I was over the hill, I was thriving. I felt so relieved not to have a fanatical coach I needed to please or scholarship obligations to fulfill. I still loved speed. I loved swimming fast. Speed is the best feeling in the world if you're going fast for yourself. But if you need to go fast for other people, everything changes. All of a sudden, you're being chased.

By that point, thankfully, my coach Michael and I had found a groove. He'd come to respect my work ethic and my need to be positive. I'd come to appreciate his steadiness, experience, and calm. Michael had even fully embraced my stretchers, Anne and Steve, and my strength coach, Andy, to the point that he was encouraging his other swimmers to seek their advice. This made me really happy. I wanted to share their expertise, not have it be something that set me apart from my team. I understood I was in a different stage of life than the other swimmers at Coral Springs. I'd worked for years. I had a child. I had resources they didn't have. But the way I saw it, I was like that older kid in the neighborhood with a driver's license and a car. What I had could be beneficial for all.

I also identified more with the younger swimmers than any of them realized. I was old enough to be a wild card again. I just wanted to get in the pool to see what my body could do.

~ ~ ~ ~ ~

In 1981, when I was 13 years old, Terry Palma, my coach on the Culver City Swim Team, took me to my first Nationals meet, at the Harvard University pool. It was the biggest event in my then short life, attended by all the athletes I worshiped in *Swimming World* magazine. During warm-ups, I tried to sneak into a lane behind Rowdy Gaines or Tracy Caulkins, the best all-around female swimmer in the country. She won Nationals in the 200-meter and 400-meter individual medleys at age 14, and set world records in both those events at age 15. I was totally in awe.

Terry had long hair and a beard, wore corduroy jeans, and drove a Volkswagen bus. I had braces, my hands appeared to be about two sizes too big for the rest of my body, and I had so much energy that if I were a kid now someone probably would have labeled me as having ADHD. But I tried to play it cool. I saw all the older swimmers listening to their Walkmans, looking super-serious as they psyched themselves up for races. So I started wearing my Walkman everywhere, trying to look serious myself as I cranked up Rick Springfield, REO Speedwagon, and Hall & Oates.

I was so young and such a rookie that when I went into the women's locker room and saw the older swimmers shaving their bodies, I had no idea what they were doing. Swimmers shave bodies to reduce drag and to have a better feel for the water. Nobody understands completely if the effects are physical or psychological or both, but after you shave your body you feel amazing, like you're sliding through the pool. Even in full-body racing suits like the LZR, swimmers still shave their whole bodies, because the suits are so tight and thin that small hairs poke through and create drag. Back then we raced in sleeveless, legless tanks—what we call practice suits now—and shaving made a huge difference. You'd dive in and feel suddenly sleek and fast. Still, at Nationals, when I saw the older girls shaving for the first time, I just ran out of the locker room. I'd never even used a razor on my legs. I was much too scared to try shaving my whole body.

Despite that, I still made the finals of the 50-yard freestyle—it was me and seven college girls. That year I was in seventh grade, and I tied for sixth at Nationals with Amy Caulkins, Tracy's sister. I was pretty stoked. Somewhere inside of me I started to realize I had the ability to be not just a good swimmer but an exceptional swimmer if I applied myself. No one made a big deal of it, especially inside my family. When I came home from Harvard my brothers' response was "Congratulations, whatever." My own response wasn't all that much more pronounced. Neither wins nor losses stay with me for long—though after that first Nationals I did train my sights on swimming faster than the girls who'd beat me in the finals, and that would mean swimming as fast as anyone in the world.

The only problem was that the 50-meter freestyle wasn't an Olympic event. The shortest swimming race in the Olympic Games was then 100 meters, and I didn't have the stamina for that. I was just that girl who could swim really fast for 25 seconds, nothing more. People liked to refer to me as a "drop dead" sprinter, meaning I'd drop dead on the back half of a 100-meter race. The label annoyed me, but I was too young to worry about it much. I was still in junior high. I didn't think further ahead than next week.

One day, around that time, I was carpooling to a swim meet with my sister, Lara, and my friend Kerry O'Mahoney. Kerry's dad was driving.

"Mr. O," I said on the way there, "I'm going to beat Sippy Woodhead in the 50 today."

Sippy Woodhead (her real name is Cynthia, but her little sister couldn't pronounce that and called her Sippy) was one of the best freestyle swimmers in the world. She'd held the world record in the 200-meter freestyle for five years. She'd even held the world record in the 50-meter freestyle for a few minutes before it was broken by Jill Sterkel the same day.

"Okay, that's great, Dara," said Mr. O'Mahoney. I'm sure he just thought I was mouthing off.

But at the meet that day I did beat Sippy Woodhead. On the way home, Mr. O'Mahoney took us to Jack in the Box for dinner.

"See, Mr. O," I said, "I did beat Sippy."

He nodded and said, "Yes, you did."

That was an early lesson for me about confidence. I believed I could do something remarkable, and my confidence helped me pull it off.

~ ~ ~ ~ ~

The next year, my long-haired, hippie-style coach Terry started shaping my workouts to focus even more on sprinting and less on endurance. We'd both grown curious to see how fast I could go. So Terry cut out "garbage yardage," as he called it. He had me swim fewer and faster sets, totaling 4,000 to 5,000 meters a day, five times a week. (Interestingly, this is about what I swim now.) When the distance swimmers on the Tandem Swim Club swam a set of ten 100s, Terry would have me do only three 100s, but a whole lot faster and with more rest in between. Not only is this how you train properly to sprint, but Terry knew me well enough to realize that if I was forced to swim too many meters, I'd just get bored and resentful and quit.

At Nationals in 1982, in Gainesville, Florida, I was 14 years old and I shaved for the first time. Then I got up on the blocks for the 50-yard freestyle alongside Jill Sterkel, who was then 21 years old and the best in the world. I touched in 22.44 seconds—and I won.

That was thrilling by itself. It also meant I'd made my first National team.

Now that I was on the National team, I had a choice of swimming in one of two international meets. I could go swim in either Spain and Germany, or France and Holland. Both trips sounded incredibly exciting, but nothing at that time was quite as exciting as Rowdy Gaines. I had a huge, overwhelming crush on Rowdy, who was then 22 years old. He'd graduated from Auburn University in 1981, retired for a few months (a lot of swimmers around that time were really disheartened after the United States boycotted the 1980 Olympics in Moscow), but then his father had convinced him to come back to the sport. Rowdy was funny, handsome, smart, charming, and very fast. I followed him everywhere I could. If my sister, Lara, was around, I'd get her to follow Rowdy with me, too, so I could pretend she had the crush, not me, but of course Rowdy knew. I had all the subtlety of a billboard that read "DARA TORRES IS IN LOVE WITH ROWDY GAINES." Rowdy signed up for the National team's France and Holland trip. So I signed up for the France and Holland trip, too.

Back then, before races, we'd all get massages with lots of oil. On the day of the finals of the 50-meter freestyle in Holland, I lay on a massage table, getting rubbed down, when Rowdy walked over and started talking to me.

"So you're racing in the 50?" he said.

All I could think was, *Oh God, he's talking to me!* I think I managed to say, "Yeah."

"What'd you do this morning?" Rowdy asked.

I told him my time in the preliminaries.

"What's the world record?"

I said, "Twenty-five seventy-one."

"Well," Rowdy said, "you'll go 25.69 tonight."

After he walked away, I tried to focus on my finals. I put on my Walkman and listened to Men at Work. Then I got up on the blocks, crouched down to start, and touched the wall in . . . 25.69 seconds.

I'd broken the world record. But mostly I couldn't wait to tell Rowdy my time.

After I warmed down, I climbed back onto the massage table to get rubbed again. Rowdy walked over.

"Well, how'd you do?" he asked in his cute, vaguely Southern accent.

I said, "I went 25.69."

He couldn't believe it.

That night was our last night in Holland. My roommate, Kim Rodenbaugh, happened to have a crush on a different guy on the National team, Tony Corbisiero. So Rowdy and Tony came by to hang out in our room—with the door open, of course, as per the code of conduct we'd all had to sign. Eventually, someone walked by and told Rowdy he had a phone call in the lobby.

"Why don't you come with me?" he asked.

So I stood with Rowdy in the lobby as he talked on the phone, becoming ever more miserable by the minute, as I convinced myself that he must be chatting with a girlfriend back home. The final straw was when I heard him say, "I love you." I couldn't take it anymore. I bolted and started running to my room. But before

I could get there, Rowdy caught up with me and planted an innocent kiss on my cheek.

That was definitely the highlight of my young life.

Even better, the whole world soon thought we were a couple. The next day, we flew to France. In the afternoon, Rowdy and I were doing some group stretches together on the pool deck (group stretches were really popular then) when a photographer from the sports newspaper *L'Equipe* took our picture. The photo ran in the paper under the headline "Le Couple Royal!" I still have the clipping, and so does Rowdy's mom.

A week later, I was deposited back at home at the Westlake School for Girls.

My classmates didn't really know what to make of me. I was that kid who swam every day after school in Culver City. I played volleyball in the fall and basketball in the winter, and I swam with the school team in the spring. Our school pool had three lanes, in which the 45 girls on the swim team trained at once. It's funny to realize now how monomaniacal I was. Even on the Westlake team, hardly a powerhouse, I was constantly asking my coach, Darlene Bible, for advice. How did my turns look? My streamlines? My starts? I was jumpy and I had no attention span for school, but Lord knows, I wanted to swim fast. My stepfather, Ed, a serious tennis player, understood the competitor in me better than anyone else in my family. "If you're a runner-up, nobody knows who you are," he told me one day. "You'll always feel like a loser if you don't win." My classmates voted me "Most Likely to Break a Record in the Guinness World Book," but mostly I think I'm remembered at Westlake as that tomboy who wore the gray polyester pants on the first day of school.

In the spring of 1983, just around my sixteenth birthday, I was sitting in a meeting of the Southern California Swimming Association, a group of coaches and swimmers in which I was an athlete representative, when Mark Schubert, the coach of the well-known swim program at Mission Viejo, slipped me a note. It said, "I hear you want to go train in Fort Lauderdale."

I wrote back, "Yes, I'm thinking about it."

After my win in the 50-yard freestyle at Nationals, my groovy coach, Terry, had started encouraging me to go swim with a bigger program and faster swimmers so I could try to improve my 100-meter freestyle time enough to make the 1984 Olympic team. The plan at the moment was for me to move to Florida and train with coach Jack Nelson alongside my friend Paige Zemina, who was also training for the 1984 Olympics.

Mark, trim and straitlaced as a military guy, wrote back, "Can I talk to you after the meeting?"

I wrote, "Yes."

Mission Viejo, Mark's team, was the coolest team around. The Mission kids always wore matching blue and yellow T-shirts and sweatpants on deck, and matching blue and yellow swimsuits and caps in the water. They all looked so strong and like they were having so much fun. But they were distance swimmers. I'd heard they swam 18,000 meters a day.

When the meeting ended, Mark pulled me aside. "Have you ever thought about coming to Mission Viejo?"

"Are you kidding?" I asked. "You guys only swim distance events. I wouldn't go there."

Mark assured me he was putting together a sprinting group, and that he'd design sprint workouts for me, meaning I'd have to swim less. There's an old saying in swimming circles: "When the going gets tough, the sprinters get out." I knew I couldn't swim 18,000 meters a day. That was nearly four times more than I was doing with Terry. But I did like the idea of being one of those cool Mission Viejo swimmers. Plus Mission Viejo was only 90 minutes from my house, as opposed to across the country, and I'd just gotten my driver's license and a car with plates that said LA SWIMR. So I said to Mark, "Okay, that sounds good. But first you have to talk to my dad."

I didn't think my father was going to like the idea of me dropping out of the tony, uniformed Westlake School for Girls to attend Mission Viejo High, where the kids all wore flip-flops and smoked in the bathroom. But Mark, undaunted and ever committed to swimming, drove over to my father's Bel Air mansion to make his case. I hadn't told him too much about my dad. I think he was pretty shocked to see the huge lawns with statues everywhere, and the housekeeper answering the door. But Mark's not easily intimidated, and he prevailed. By that point, he'd honed his coaching style and hardly ever screamed. All his swimmers swam 9,000 meters in the morning and 9,000 meters in the afternoon, with Mark saying little more than, "Will the ladies in lane four please do 24 hundreds on 1:05?" He'd ask for 500 sit-ups in the same, placid way. He was like a drill sergeant conducting boot camp without raising his voice.

Around that time my mother also wrote my father a letter, encouraging him to let me go. She reminded him that Mission Viejo was much closer than Florida. She'd be able to visit me on weekends, and I truly did need world-class coaching and stiffer competition if I was going to continue to improve. So at the end of my sophomore year at Westlake, I moved down to Mission Viejo and into the home of Mike and Flo Stutzman, who'd offered to be my host parents for the year. They had a six-year-old son, Sean, and a 10-year-old daughter, Heather, who swam on the Mission Viejo junior swim team. I loved the Stutzmans immediately. I got to make my own breakfast and lunch. Flo made me dinner and taught me how to iron shirts.

I had a much harder time adjusting to the Mission Viejo practices than life away from home. With Terry, I was used to goofing off, hanging on the lane lines, sitting on the bottom of the pool if I didn't want to hear him boss me around. Mark had no truck with monkey business. During a kick set, you couldn't turn and talk to the swimmer next to you, or you'd have to get out and do push-ups. You absolutely could not cheat. Mark was ginger with me at the beginning. He knew I was new to his type of discipline, and that he couldn't let me enter what he called "the valley of fatigue." His distance swimmers lived in that state of exhaustion, as they needed to break down regularly to build up endurance. But Mark understood my fundamental nature as a sprinter, both mentally and physically. My goal at Mission Viejo was to learn how to swim a fast 100 meters without dying on the last 30 meters. I also needed to grow up a little and acquire a work ethic—and that's where Mark's authoritarian skills came in.

One day, I can't remember why, Mark and I got in a big fight in practice, so big that I ran off the pool deck, into my car, and started driving. Mark followed me on foot and we had a ridiculous chase in the parking lot, me trying to find a way to escape, Mark blocking off my wagon with his body. Eventually, he managed to corner me near the lot's entrance, which had a row of those one-way spikes that pop your tires if you drive across them in the wrong direction. By that point, we were both laughing over our ridiculous showdown. It was way too dramatic and obvious even to me that I needed to get back to the pool. I knew I had nothing to gain by driving away. Mark had made me see that I was responsible for my own failure—or if I wanted to, I could be responsible for my own success.

So I parked and walked back to practice. I stopped climbing out of the pool when sets got too hard. I started doing every stroke and every meter Mark requested. That showdown in the parking lot forced me to realize that I wanted to grow up as a swimmer. I wanted to reach my potential. Mark's primary lesson had gotten through to me: By cheating in practice I was cheating myself.

When Mark took the job at Mission Viejo in 1972, he was 25 years old and Mission Viejo had never even won the Orange County Swim Conference. Two years later, in 1974, Mission Viejo was the national champion. Mark believed then, as he still does, that you choose your level of achievement by choosing the level of your expectations. Mark did everything for his team, always, and he expected no less from his swimmers. In 1973, he noticed that the East Germans in the World Championships in Belgrade were wearing "skin suits" made of a single layer of stretchy nylon. He came home and ordered skin suits for his team. Mark locked the gate to practice so nobody could show up late. He catered meals at meets to make sure we all ate well. He told us not to wear dark caps on hot sunny days, because the dark colors trapped heat and depleted strength. He set curfews and enforced them.

I needed the structure Mark provided, particularly at age 16. Adolescence can be a scary time for female swimmers, as lots of young girls set national and world records but fail to remain dominant as adults. Part of the reason is that girls' bodies don't have much bulk. Their strength-to-weight ratio is really good. But with puberty comes change, and change is terrifying if you're used to the machine of your own body performing a certain way. For male swimmers, like male gymnasts, puberty is almost entirely positive. You enter puberty a little pip-squeak and come out taller, leaner, stronger, and almost always faster. But for female swimmers, like female gymnasts, puberty is not always a plus. You often enter adolescence with a sleek, strong, powerful, and hydrodynamic body. You come out with hips, breasts, thighs, and a much higher percentage of body fat, all of which can slow you down.

That first summer at Mission Viejo, at age 16, I broke the world record in the 50-meter freestyle again, lowering it to 25.62 seconds. Six months later, in January 1984, I swam a 100-meter freestyle in 56.64, improving my personal-best time by over half a second. During my year with Mark at Mission Viejo I learned how to work hard out of the pool, too. He asked us to do 500 sit-ups a day. I did 700. I ran two to four miles after practice in addition to all my swimming and lifting weights. One day in the spring of 1984, just a few months before Olympic Trials that year, Mark warmed us up in the pool with a "ladder" of successive sprints—50 meters, 100 meters, 150 meters, 200 meters, 250 meters, 200 meters, 150 meters, 100 meters, and 50 meters—each with 20 seconds of rest in between.

"Build with each one! Build stronger with each one!" Mark shouted as we started off.

That warm-up was nearly as long as my entire practices had been with Terry. When I finished the ladder, I was already tired. Then Mark gave us our main set: nine diving sprints at maximum effort—three 25 meters, three 75 meters, and three 125 meters.

After the first 125-meter sprint, my legs felt like noodles. My kick was faltering. I felt like I was breaking down. "You're using a broken tempo kick," Mark chastised me.

"I know, but . . ." I crumpled my legs under me to show him how tired they were.

"This is where you've got to make yourself do it," Mark said to me firmly. No one relishes pain, but I did appreciate Mark's sternness. "Better die now than, uh, later, right?"

He meant in the back half of the 100-meter freestyle at Olympic Trials, when every tenth and hundredth of a second would really count.

~ ~ ~ ~ ~

In 1984, Olympic Trials were in Indianapolis. I was 17. At that point, those Trials were the most nerve-racking swim meet I'd experienced.

For the past year, at the Stutzmans' house, I'd had a sign over my bed: "26.4 + 28.4 = 54.8," my ideal splits for 100 meters. I'd improved a lot under Mark's stern guidance, but I was still not a shoo-in on the Olympic team. I was racing only in the 100-meter freestyle. If I finished in the top two, I'd swim in the individual 100-meter freestyle in the Olympics in Los Angeles. If I finished in the top four, I'd swim on the 4 × 100-meter freestyle relay team. But back then, due to the rules of Olympic relay team selection, nothing was for sure. At any point during Olympic Trials a swimmer could "challenge," meaning that at the end of each day's events the swimmer could ask for a time trial. If that swimmer swam faster than any of the other girls already on the relay, the slowest person then on the relay would be kicked off.

After the preliminaries in the 100-meter freestyle, the first event of the meet, I was seeded third. Before the finals that evening I'd gotten a manicure, and I showed up on the blocks with my fingernails on each hand painted "5" "4" "." "8" in yellow and blue. I felt the whole world was watching. I crouched and listened for the starting signal. The race was over before I knew it.

I swam my 100 meters in 56.36 seconds, touching fourth.

I'd missed a spot in the individual 100-meter freestyle—I was heartbroken about that. But at least I was going to the Olympics. I had a spot on the relay. For now.

But there were still five days left of Olympic Trials, and on the last night Tracy Caulkins decided to challenge for my spot on the 4 × 100-meter freestyle relay. She already had spots on the Olympic team in four events, but if she swam faster than 56.36 seconds she'd swim in the relay, too. As the fifth fastest, I'd be dropped down into an alternate position. I'd attend the Games but likely miss my chance at a gold medal. I'd maybe even miss out on breaking a world record.

I could not bear to watch Tracy swim. Just as she slipped off her sweat clothes, I put on my Walkman, turned Men at Work up to full volume, and ran into the women's locker room under the stands. I slumped to the floor in the corner. I held my legs and started moaning, "Oh God, oh God, oh God."

When it was over, Tracy did not beat my time. I was extremely grateful to Mark for not letting me sit on the bottom of the pool or allowing me to run out of practice. I'd needed him to work me as hard as he did. The clock doesn't care if you're tired, or hungry, or uninspired, or if your legs hurt after the ladder. Swimming rewards hard work and discipline. As Mark used to say to his swimmers all the time, "No excuse in the world counts for squat." Nothing you can say can change your time—56.36 seconds is 56.36 seconds. No amount of wishful thinking is going to make it 54.8.

9

~ ~ ~ ~ ~

On Performing
Under Pressure

Olympic Trials are pretty much the scariest swim meets in the world. They're even scarier than the Olympics themselves. At the Olympics, you feel great just for being there. You're representing your country. You're one of the best athletes in the world. But at Trials for the Olympics, if you don't swim fast enough, you disappear. Most people don't pay any attention to swimming other than at the Olympics. Also, at Trials you're constantly worrying that if you don't swim fast, your parents are going to lose a lot of money on those plane tickets they bought last month when they thought they'd be going to watch you compete in the Olympic Games.

Olympic Trials were scheduled for the end of June and the beginning of July 2008, and in the month leading up to them I started to taper down how much I was swimming. All swimmers decrease their yardage before big meets. The idea is for your body to be fully rested when your performance counts most. So instead of swimming 40,000 meters a week (7,000 or 8,000 meters a day, six days a week) or, in my case, 25,000 meters (5,000 meters a day, five days a week), a swimmer might cut down to swimming just a third or a half of that. How hard you work out decreases, too. You focus more on recovery, on longer periods of lower-intensity exercise meant to flush every bit of that burn-inducing lactic acid out of your muscles. Gone are the exhausting high-intensity "quality" workouts. Even sprinters don't sprint much. By the time you start tapering, the grueling work of preparing your body to race is already over. You've either done your job—built up your body to be the fastest—or you haven't done your job. You're like a carpenter who's hammered the last nail into a house. All that's left to do is paint.

One of a coach's most important roles is tapering his swimmers properly, to make sure each is in position to swim his or her fastest at the optimal time. Some swimmers drop seconds off their best times in practice after tapering; others only drop a tenth or two. But at meets like Olympic Trials every tenth counts—heck, every hundredth counts. At Trials it doesn't matter if you've set a new American record, or even a new world record, the week or month before. If you don't swim fast there, you don't make the Olympic team. And it's little consolation that a poorly managed taper is probably to blame.

Like a lot of elite swimmers, I always say tapering is my favorite part of the swimming season, but that's only partially true. The reality is that I spend most of my tapers feeling horrible and sluggish, and when I'm not feeling horrible and sluggish I'm cranky and agitated, unsure how to blow off all that extra steam I usually leave in the pool. Taper is a really confusing time; it's the unsettling calm before the storm. All you're supposed to do is eat, sleep, swim, and rest, not lift heavy objects, not even climb stairs unless you really have to. You try to avoid any activity outside the pool.

This works fine for the 99.9 percent of elite swimmers who don't have toddlers. But Tessa was two years old just before Trials. She didn't care much about my taper. She still wanted to be thrown around the playground and lifted in and out of her car seat and her bed. I could have tried (and probably failed) to convince her otherwise, but I decided just to give in.

I've always felt that being a mother is mostly positive for me as an athlete. Tessa keeps me focused without my becoming obsessed, so I figured even during taper she was doing more good for my spirit than harm to my body. That became especially true the closer I got to Trials. In the lead-up to that meet, more and more articles on me started appearing in national magazines. NBC started teasing my story in their pre-Olympic coverage on TV. I felt more eyes watching me every day. My BlackBerry also started buzzing every two minutes with good-luck messages from people I hadn't seen in years.

Don't get me wrong: I appreciated the support. But the attention caused me anxiety, too. I'd started swimming again for the most personal reason I can think of: because I was pregnant. I kept swimming, in many ways, because my body could still swim fast. I'd never really intended to become a hero to middle-aged athletes, and I didn't really know how well-suited I was for the job. I didn't—and still don't—think of myself as somebody who's inspiring, as somebody who's figured out any big secrets about life. I have a few basic rules that I live by: Eat well. Sleep well. Make a schedule and stick to it. Don't cheat with bad form. But mostly I tend to think of myself as someone who knows how to work hard yet is just bumbling along, trying to get the most out of my days like anybody else on earth.

In the spring heading into Trials, some days I'd feel confident; other days, my courage would flag. I worried that the increased expectations generated by the media would interfere with my performance, that I'd short-circuit under the pressure as I sometimes had in my prime. If I was going to swim my fastest, I needed to calm down. I needed to feel that I was going to win. So I drove back over to Bernard's modest coral-colored bungalow to consult my medium again. As always, in his office, I wrote down the names of three dead people and three more questions, this time including "Am I going to medal in an individual event in the 2008 Olympic Games?" (Bernard would always say, "Ask vague, receive vague. Ask specific, get specific." He was referring to the kinds of answers he'd give.) Bernard left the room, came back, placed the card I had folded while he was away on his forehead. Then he started talking one more time to his connections over there in the spirit world. He told me, in his cryptic way, that I'd medal in the Olympics, but he said this would happen only if I believed in myself every single day.

I've taken lots of people in my life to see Bernard. Most walk into his blue-carpeted office feeling skeptical, and usually Bernard wins them over. Before Bernard retired to work as a medium, he was a steelworker. He made his way up from the lowest pay grade to a fairly high one in his factory. He used his powers of insight to troubleshoot the ovens used for melting iron into steel. Bernard has seen me through all kinds of hard passages—infertility, divorce, Olympics—but even for someone who wants to believe as much as I do, a guy who talks to dead people can provide only so much comfort. Despite Bernard's reassurance, I continued to worry. What if I got up on the blocks at Olympic Trials and my 41-year-old body seized up? What if I false started?

Complicating matters, Michael, my coach, was a mess. A few months earlier, he'd herniated a disc in his back. He'd thought he'd recovered, or at least he told me he'd recovered. But then, in mid-June, two week before Trials in Omaha, the disc exploded. He was in unbelievable pain. He couldn't walk across the pool deck without sitting down. Naturally, he didn't want to abandon his swimmers, so Michael took handfuls of painkillers and kept showing up for practice. Later I would find out what was really wrong, and I'd kick myself for not realizing he was not just wiped out due to pain. His health problems extended way beyond his back. But that spring, when I'd see Michael at the Coral Springs pool, I just thought he was whacked out on Percocet, even when he spent nearly the entire two hours slumped in a plastic chair.

One day, a week before Trials, I showed up at practice, stashed my gym bag in the shade and my water bottle under my starting block. Then Michael handed me a workout that called for almost 4,000 meters, including twelve 100s, aerobic pace. By that point in our relationship, I'd accepted Michael's authority completely. He'd still tease me, calling me the queen, or diva, often going out of his way to refer to some older diva, like Judi Dench, but generally I did what he said. He'd made it possible for me to get here. He'd understood exactly what I'd needed to do to succeed mentally and physically. He'd drawn more out of me in a 40-something postpartum body than anybody ever had produced in me in my teens, twenties, or thirties. I've had the honor of working with a lot of amazing coaches in my life, but for me, at this time in my life, Michael was the best. He understood that I drive myself hard. He knew his job was to steer.

But that morning, the workout Michael gave me looked insane. A 4,000-meter workout was far more than what I thought I should do.

"What the F is this?" I asked. (I'd tried to stop swearing for Tessa's sake, so I resorted to first initials.) "I'm not going to do this! I'm swimming in a little over a week."

Michael may have been drugged, but he was also a seasoned coach. So he just sat in his plastic chair, watching me flip out, as

I'm sure he'd watched plenty of other swimmers flip out during taper before.

"What do you mean?" he asked, clearly enjoying my display of nerves.

"It says here I'm supposed to do twelve 100s. Don't you think that's a little much? How many of those pills are you taking?"

"It's none of your business, and no, I don't think that's too much," Michael replied, his voice tired but firm. He reminded me I was going to need to swim six times over four days at Olympic Trials, in the preliminaries, semifinals, and finals for both the 50-meter and 100-meter freestyle.

Michael looked gray and awful, but he kept his gaze steady on me. "You need to keep up your conditioning right now."

~ ~ ~ ~ ~

The last Sunday in June 2008 I spent at home, packing, in Parkland, Florida, trying to remain rested and calm while Tessa bounced off the walls. Olympic Trials started that night, but my first race wasn't until the Thursday of that week, so Michael and I had come up with a plan: I'd arrive in Omaha late, on Monday afternoon, after almost all the other athletes. I'd hold back a little in the preliminaries and the semifinals of both the 50- and the 100-meter freestyle. Then, in the finals of both races, I'd surprise the world with what my 41-year-old body could do.

Very few people knew how fast I was capable of swimming, because I'd raced only sparingly in the past year. I don't like to swim "build-up" races just to gain experience. You don't taper before those meets, so you don't often swim your best times, and that tends to make me feel worse as the season progresses instead of more confident. I also didn't want to race too often because that 100-percent effort takes its toll. I'd recovered well from my shoulder and knee surgeries in the late fall and winter, but I'd developed some other problems in a different part of my shoulder. Specifically, I'd developed some arthritis in my acromioclavicular, or AC, joint, the joint at the top of the shoulder that connects the highest part of the scapula to the clavicle. (This joint enables you to lift your arm over your head, a major part of the freestyle stroke.) Through the spring I had several cortisone shots to relieve the pain, including one just a few weeks before Trials. I worried that too much racing would make the problem worse, and I certainly didn't have time to have my AC joint surgically repaired before the Olympic Trials or Games.

Since Nationals in 2007 I'd competed only once in the 100-meter freestyle, and four times in the 50-meter freestyle. In May, at the Texas Senior Circuit, I'd gone 54.17 seconds in the 100-meter freestyle and 24.56 seconds in the 50. I felt good about my times—the 54.17 was a personal best, and I felt confident I could bring my 50-meter time even lower. Yet given how little I'd raced, I didn't feel rock solid. I knew I could swim faster than my competitors realized, but I'd also have to keep my head together if I was going to perform my best when it counted.

That April, I'd turned 41 and Tessa had turned two. Her primary interests in life were Elmo, Dora the Explorer, and riding her toy plastic car between the SUV and the Mini Cooper in the garage, while standing up. She was just like me in so many ways: constantly moving, challenging everybody and everything in sight. Sometimes I'd watch her on the video screen of her baby monitor when she was supposed to be taking a nap. She'd be scrambling like mad, trying to climb out of her crib. Then I'd make a few loud noises like I was going to walk into her room. Immediately, she'd plop down and pretend to be asleep.

Tessa understood that Mommy swam. (My stretcher Anne had taught her to say, "Mommy's fast, Daddy's smart.") She even knew that Mommy had some important swimming to do soon. But she didn't really know, or care, what that important swimming was or where it was going to take place—if it was going to be in the tiny dipping pool in our backyard, or at Coral Springs, or what. Like all two-year-olds, Tessa lived entirely in the present. She didn't worry about the past or the future. I wished I could say that for myself.

"Mommy, you swim," she said when we sat down on the couch in the living room with David to watch the first night of Trials. "Mommy, you swim! You swim fast!"

In Tessa's innocence I felt all my fears. What if I didn't swim fast? For the past 18 months I'd worked so hard and, increasingly, so publicly. I knew I was capable of swimming faster than I had in my life, but still, the fact that so many people were watching made me extremely nervous. I had also started worrying about the logistics involved if I *did* make the team. If I swam well at Trials, I'd be flying straight from Omaha to a training camp in California. From there I'd fly with the Olympic team directly to Singapore, where we'd acclimate to the heat and time (Beijing and Singapore are in the same time zone) and train some more. If I swam well at Trials, I wouldn't be home, or even share a hotel room with Tessa, for seven weeks. USA Swimming rules forbid family members from entering athletes' hotel rooms. The rules were written with athletes' parents in mind, but they were the rules nonetheless.

That night as we watched the big, beautiful pool in the Qwest Center in Omaha, Nebraska, on TV, Tessa kept saying, over and over, "Mommy, you swim. You swim fast!" My flight was in the morning, but the truth is I would have put on my LZR racing suit and dived through our hi-def TV set had that been an option. My anxiety was mounting by the minute. There was only one cure: to get out there and swim. That night, Michael Phelps and Ryan Lochte placed one and two in the finals of the men's 400-meter individual medley. No one ever doubted that they'd make the team. Still, they'd done it. They were going to the 2008 Olympics in Beijing. I was beside myself with envy.

~ ~ ~ ~ ~

Whatever else anybody might have to say about Omaha, that city really knows how to throw a swim meet. What makes it even more amazing is that Omaha doesn't even have a permanent Olympic-size pool.

For Trials, Omaha installed in the Qwest Center two gigantic, spectacular versions of those crummy aboveground pools people sometimes stick in their backyards. Combined, the pools held two million gallons of water. The competition pool had ten 50-meter lanes and was eight and a half feet deep. The warm-up pool, in a separate area, had eight 50-meter lanes plus eight more 25-meter lanes that stuck off the side to make the pool form an L, a really great setup for swimmers. More impressive, the mood in the Qwest Center was electric. They played terrific music. They blasted off fireworks each time a swimmer broke a record in the finals. Nearly 12,000 spectators showed up each day. The announcers called the races at the tops of their lungs, screaming, usually for Michael Phelps, "HE'S AHEAD OF WORLD-RECORD PACE!!!!" Mark Schubert, who's coached at every Olympics since 1984 and been to every great pool in the world, called the Qwest Center "literally the best swimming venue" he'd ever seen. Too bad it's gone. After Olympic Trials ended, chemicals were added to the pool to neutralize the chlorine, and the Omaha Fire Department pumped the two million gallons of water out of the pools through fire hoses into a nearby lake. The Myrtha Pools company then disassembled the decks, blocks, gutters, walls, buttresses, bands, and liners, and carted away the pools.

On the last Monday morning in June, I kissed Tessa good-bye, trying not to freak her out too much. I couldn't believe how long I might be gone. My hope was to take the separation one step at a time. Anne, Steve, and I drove to the Fort Lauderdale airport. They were traveling with me to Omaha, and if we got that far, to California, Singapore, and Beijing. While we were waiting for our plane, I kept my iPod on. I needed to stay relaxed and loose. Of course, I also fiddled with my BlackBerry, as I always do, and there at the gate I saw an e-mail from a swimmer friend who was already at Trials.

She'd attached a picture showing a huge poster of me on the door leading into the Qwest Center. At first I thought this must be a joke. Just the day before, the *New York Times Magazine* had run a full-page photograph of me in a bikini. The photographer had used really strong lighting that made the muscles in my abs pop out. Everybody I knew (and lots of people I didn't) seemed to be commenting on what they called my "12-pack," and that made me self-conscious. On our flight to Omaha I tried to put those images out of my mind. But when we arrived, there it was: a nearly life-size picture of me on the door leading into the pool.

My heart started racing. Clearly, the strategy of sneaking into Trials under the radar was not going off as planned. For weeks I'd been hoping I'd feel less stressed once I dove into the warm-up pool at Trials. I hoped that being in the water would make me feel like I was at just another swim meet, like so many I'd been to before. So I dropped my bags in my hotel room, which was part of the convention center, and I headed down to the pool. I deck-changed into my practice suit (towel around my waist, sweatpants off, suit bottom on, arms out of T-shirt armholes, suit top on, T-shirt off). I pulled on my Coral Springs swim cap. Then I dove in.

I felt awful. Positively awful.

Not regular awful, like I think I'm going to throw up, as I do before every meet. I felt like a rock—stiff, dense, and heavy. Really, really bad. I thought, at first, I must just be rigid from sitting on airplanes. So I sent text messages to Anne and Steve and asked them to come over and stretch me in my hotel room that night.

"How do I feel?" I asked Anne as she mashed my muscles with her feet. "Do I feel stiff?" I'd felt so crappy in the pool.

"Uhhhh . . . ," Anne stalled. "You feel . . . ah . . . really good. Yeah . . . you feel good."

It was the least convincing "good" I had ever heard.

The next day, I woke up still feeling stiff. I went back down to the warm-up pool and swam an easy couple thousand meters. That didn't work.

Rowdy Gaines stopped by to give me some encouragement. We'd stayed close friends after my insane childhood crush. Before me, Rowdy had been the oldest swimmer to qualify for Olympic Trials, at age 35. This year Susan Rapp von der Lippe, who'd won a silver medal in the 200-meter breaststroke in the 1984 Olympic Games, was also competing. She'd qualified in the 100-meter breaststroke and the 100-meter butterfly. She was a year older than me, she had two kids, ages 9 and 12, and she'd only trained three days a week. Her goal had been to qualify for Trials, not to make the Olympic team (she was ranked 79th in the breaststroke and 112th in the butterfly). She was happy just to be here. Lately she'd been telling the press she hoped just to blend in here in Omaha and not "gross anybody out with [her] 40-year-old mommy's body." But neither Rowdy's long-standing friendship nor Susan's perspective and humor calmed me down.

Neither did the fact that my entire family had flown into town, including some of my brothers who hadn't seen me swim in person since I was a kid. The problem was my BlackBerry, which I probably should have thrown to the bottom of the pool. (If I ever swim at Trials again, please remind me to do that.) The dang phone was now vibrating incessantly with messages from friends and fans, and I was too addicted to texting to turn it off. For the first time in my 24-year athletic career, people outside the small swimming world seemed to know who I was and to care how I performed. I was flattered, but I didn't know how to cope. I was used to being known only to die-hard swimming fans. Now I was becoming the hero of anybody who didn't want to hang up a dream just because she'd become a mother, or who didn't want the date on the calendar to tell her when it was time to give up.

That night, Tuesday, Anne called me on my cell phone from her hotel room down the hall. "Oh my God, oh my God! You're on *Pardon the Interruption!*"

I could hear the TV blaring in the background. ESPN's *Pardon the Interruption* was Anne's favorite show. "This is incredible! This is just totally the coolest thing!" she kept screaming.

I wished I shared her enthusiasm. I loved Anne and I loved her spirit, but my brain felt like it was going to explode. I couldn't deal with being on people's television sets. I couldn't deal with the increased expectations. Finally, I cut her off midsentence. "Anne, I can't take it. I don't want to hear it right now."

That's when it clicked: I felt horrible in the water because I didn't know how to handle this. I was letting myself get weighed down by the outside world.

The next morning, Wednesday, I swam a little and still felt stiff and miserable. I was now extremely nervous. My first race was the next day.

I've always been a swimmer who puts a great deal of stock in how I feel in warm-up. I depend on the physical and mental reassurance of feeling perfectly prepared. But in less than 24 hours I was swimming in the preliminaries of the 100-meter freestyle at Olympic Trials and I had no faith in my body. Clearly, that faith wasn't going to arrive by doing a few more laps. So I retreated to my hotel room with Anne, Steve, and Julie Stupp, a teammate from Coral Springs. We ordered a dumb movie on pay-per-view. I hoped that would calm me down.

But as the movie started, I felt like I couldn't breathe. I couldn't sit still. I was about to burst into tears. "I'll be right back!" I tried to say as normally as I could. Then I grabbed my BlackBerry and I left.

My room happened to be right by the elevators, at the beginning of an extremely long hallway. I walked all the way down to the opposite end, where there was a window. I sat down and started crying.

I don't know how to describe it: I wasn't sad. I was emotionally overloaded. I felt every feeling you can imagine all at once. Fear, check. Happiness, check. Pride, check. But more than anything else, I felt watched. It's funny: Athletes crave recognition, but most sports, in the end, are solitary pursuits. You compete because you want to. You win because you have a burning need to be the best. But now my swimming felt bigger than I did. I felt millions of eyes on me. I was no longer the only one invested in how I performed in the pool.

That my effort to make a fifth Olympic team had become a vessel for other people's hopes and dreams was beautiful—I realized that. But it also felt strange. Swimming had never been like this for me before. In just the past two hours I'd received phone, e-mail, and text messages from people who'd told me they'd started running again, or cycling again, or gone back to school because they'd heard I was still swimming at age 41. The pride I felt was amazing, but so was the fear. What if I sparked all that hope and then swam slowly? I hate to disappoint people. I've been trying to avoid disappointing people my whole life. Now there were so many more people to disappoint than ever before.

I didn't have a plan when I sat down at the end of that long hallway. I knew I needed to talk to somebody, but I didn't want to call my mother or Tessa's father, David, or a close friend. I was too upset. I knew I'd scare them and I'd probably become completely unglued. So I did something that might seem really strange. I called my orthopedic surgeon, Dr. Chalal. My shoulder had been bothering me anyway, and Dr. Chalal was used to talking to athletes in vulnerable situations. Besides, he's funny, sarcastic, and he hardly ever sleeps. I figured he'd hear me out and settle me down.

I'm sure he thought I was nuts, but God bless that guy, he just rolled with my call and made me feel like my reaching out to him was the most normal thing in the world. Just connecting to someone outside the Qwest Center was a huge relief. Besides, Chalal wasn't emotionally invested in my performance. He referred to himself as the handyman who fixed my joints. He just told me everything would be fine and that he had total confidence in me—exactly what I needed to hear.

Then, while I was talking to Dr. Chalal, Mark Schubert walked to the end of the hall where I was sitting.

Mark, as it turned out, had one of the last rooms on the corridor, just across from where I planted myself. When I finished talking to the doctor, I couldn't remember which door Mark had entered, so I called his cell.

"Aren't you right outside my door?" he asked me.

I said, "Yeah."

He came out and sat down next to me on the floor, both of us leaning against the wall, our knees bent straight up, like we were kids hanging out in front of our lockers at school. I needed that so badly at that moment—to feel like a kid again with my childhood coach.

I told Mark about all the pressure I was feeling, and he, wise as ever, told me to tune it out. I'd started swimming again for myself. I'd kept swimming because I wanted to—it made me happy and gave meaning to my life. "Remember the joy in your own swimming," Mark told me in that same stern, gravelly voice I've been hearing since I was 16. We had a few laughs about the time he had to chase me around the parking lot at Mission Viejo. "You've worked hard for this your whole life. You went to practice. You made this happen. Let your fans worry about themselves."

When I returned to my hotel room, the pay-per-view movie was over and Anne, Steve, and Julie had left. I felt a little calmer. I sat down on the edge of the bed and summoned all my will. Bernard, the medium, had told me that I'd make the Olympic team and even medal at the Olympic Games as long as I continued to believe in myself. So I committed myself to believing I could win, no matter how I felt. I also committed to following Mark's advice. Mark had been right when I was a kid: I'd needed to learn some discipline. And he was right now that I was an adult: I needed to get back in touch with my love of my sport.

I also believed I was the fastest woman at the Qwest Center. I just needed to hang on to that confidence when I was on the blocks.

The morning of the preliminaries of the 100-meter freestyle, I met my German coach, Michael from Coral Springs, down at the warm-up pool. His herniated disc had not yet been fixed. He still looked terrible, and I hate to sound like a broken record, but I still felt terrible, too. I kept muttering to myself, "Oh, God," and hoping the moment would pass.

Michael had me swimming over in the short-course section of the warm-up pool. He stood on deck, grimacing, timing me with one of his stopwatches, and shaking his head. I didn't ask for my times, because I never want to know my times before I race. They just make me compare what I'm doing that day to what I did before all the other races I've ever swum before, and mostly I find reasons to feel bad. All I want to hear from my coach before a race is a straightforward reminder like "Think about your body position on your turn." Ideally, I want to hear "You look great. You're ready to go."

Michael didn't tell me my times; he knew better at that point. He didn't tell me anything, but I could see on his face that something more than his back was bothering him.

"Hey, is this 25 yards or 25 meters?" I called out to one of the other coaches standing on deck. Yards are shorter than meters, so swimming a lap in a 25-yard pool takes less time.

"Yards," the other coach yelled.

The look on Michael's face turned from confusion to grief.

I knew my times must be really bad.

Any peace of mind I'd gained in the hallway from Mark evaporated right there. I was really freaking out—not quite panicking as I had at the 1984 Olympics, but I was getting close. I dried off, pulled on my sweats, and lay down on a bunch of yoga mats so Anne and Steve could give me a quick 20-minute stretch before my race. As I was prone, contorted, and trying not to hyperventilate, Michael hobbled over.

"It's meters," he said, ashen as ever but looking relieved. "That lane you swam in this morning—it's meters."

"Thank God," I said. Swimming a lap in a 25-meter pool takes me about two whole seconds longer than swimming a lap in a pool that's 25 yards.

Michael said, "Yeah, thank God."

Of course, there was still the problem that I didn't feel good in the water, but I wasn't going to get this far and scratch my race. So with 30 minutes to go, I found an empty bathroom and pulled on my LZR racer. I couldn't believe I was swimming in an Olympic Trials again. This time, instead of a manicure with "5" "4" "." "8" on my fingernails, as I'd had in 1984, I had a pedicure of fishes on my toes. They were all blue. I chose the color to represent first place.

My plan was not to go all out. I was worried about my shoulder and my recovery time, and I needed to conserve some speed for finals. I put on my iPod and headed over to the ready room to wait for my race. On deck I splashed water on my arms and face. At the long whistle I mounted my block. At the short series of whistles I bent down in my track start, with my left leg forward and my right leg back, taking full advantage of the slight incline. At the starting signal I dove in—finally!—and swam my 100 meters in 54.47 seconds. I placed third behind Natalie Coughlin and Lacey Nymeyer.

I still didn't feel good physically, but my swim hadn't been so bad.

The semifinals that night followed the exact same pattern. I felt awful in warm-up, but in my race I swam pretty well. This time I touched in 53.76 seconds, the first time I'd ever broken 54 seconds.

Before the finals the next evening, I kept thinking about Bernard, who'd told me I just needed to believe. My coach Michael and I decided that for the finals I should swim my fastest for the entire 100 meters, instead of going all out for the first 50 meters, pulling back for 25 meters, and then gunning for the wall. But more than any particular strategy, I needed to swim my own race and not worry about anybody else. I'd lost the lead in the 100-meter freestyle at the Olympic Trials in 2000 by looking for Jenny Thompson. So now, for the 100-meter freestyle at this Olympic Trials, I pulled out those bug-eyed goggles my old hippie coach Terry Palma had duct-taped when I was 14 years old. He'd basically turned them into horse blinders, like those a Thoroughbred might wear in the Kentucky Derby. I didn't know how many more swims I had in them. The foam around the eyepieces kept coming off and I'd repeatedly reattached it with Krazy Glue. Still, I brought them with me out to the blocks, where the starter again blew the first series of short whistles to tell us to get ready. Then he blew the second long whistle for us to take our marks. At the starting signal I dove in and swam my own race. I didn't look at anybody. When I touched, I had no idea who had won.

Next to me I could see that Natalie Coughlin was smiling, so I assumed she'd placed first. I pulled off my goggles to look up at the scoreboard, but my old eyes wouldn't come into focus. I blinked and squinted . . . finally the scoreboard became clear.

Hey, wait a minute . . . , I remember thinking. *I won!*

I'd won the 100-meter freestyle at Olympic Trials. That was something I'd been trying to do for 24 years. I hugged Natalie and Lacey, who'd placed second and third. Then I swam over to the side and climbed out to kiss Michael. He looked ecstatic for the first time in months, but it was the expression on the face of Chris Jackson, my former Masters coach, that really stays with me. I'd met him as a pregnant lady who didn't swim. He was totally in shock.

"You just won the 100 freestyle at Olympic Trials!" he said to me.

"Yeah, I know!" I said.

I was so happy, and so relieved. I was not going to let anyone down.

~ ~ ~ ~ ~

Of course, I still had to swim the 50-meter freestyle, so I couldn't relax too much. But once I'd taken first in the 100-meter freestyle, my whole body changed. Anne and Steve couldn't believe the difference. Every fiber of my being had been tense, and now everything was easing up. Anne finally admitted how rigid I'd felt that Monday night. She knows how my body is supposed to feel almost as well as I do. She said she'd never felt my muscles that tight.

The preliminaries of the 50-meter freestyle were the morning after the finals of the 100-meter freestyle—a pretty tough schedule for an old lady like me. Michael really wanted me to take it easy in that first 50, which turned out to be harder than I'd thought. The preliminaries take place over several heats, and in the one before mine a swimmer named Lara Jackson from the University of Arizona broke my American record, touching in 24.50 seconds. Still, I followed my coach's advice: I held back and didn't swim full speed. But that evening, in the first heat of the semifinals, Jessica Hardy, a 21-year-old from Long Beach, California, broke the American record again.

By that point, Michael knew I couldn't stomach holding back again. So I went all out. In the semifinals I touched in 24.38 seconds. I took back the American record. This was my best time ever, but Michael was not pleased about my swim. My stroke looked great, he told me, but my start had been so bad he'd nearly fallen off his chair.

So after I had warmed down and gotten stretched, Michael made me join him in the USA Swimming booth to review the video of my race. He was right: I'd just kind of dropped into the pool. My body wasn't in a tight streamlined position. My core was lax and my limbs were sloppy, meaning I couldn't shoot through the water to the surface and start my stroke. All the other girls were nearly a body length ahead by the time I rose and started swimming.

Nobody else was in the competition arena when Michael and I finished watching the tapes. We could have turned out the lights. Originally, we'd planned for me to sleep late the next morning so I'd be rested for the finals. But now Michael wanted me back early at the warm-up pool. I needed more work on my start.

I had a hard time dozing off after such an adrenaline-filled day—Lara's breaking my American record, Jessica's breaking Lara's, then my winning the record back again. I think I managed to sleep only about four hours. In the morning, I dragged myself out of bed and met Michael back at the pool.

I swam only about 300 meters. The rest of the time we worked on my body position off the blocks.

"I don't want you thinking about anything else except your start," Michael told me repeatedly as we prepped for my last race. "Don't even think about swimming. Only think about your start."

I did my whole prerace routine—warming up, stretching, putting on racing suit, listening to iPod—thinking only about the shape of my body off those blocks. I walked out to the ready room thinking about my start. I took off my T-shirt and adjusted my cap and goggles on deck, thinking only about my start.

After this race, Trials would be over. On the blocks I curled my toes with the blue fishes painted on them over the metal edge. I'd already made the Olympic team, but the 50-meter freestyle was my race. It's the yardstick by which I judge myself. I wanted to see what I could still do.

I listened for the signal. My start was okay—not fantastic, but not that bad. I touched in 24.25 seconds, 1.64 seconds faster than I'd swum when I broke the world record 26 years earlier.

I won, setting a new American record. I'd kept my cool and swum my best.

Trials were over; now on to training camp. All I had to worry about, or so I thought, was preparing for Beijing.

10

~ ~ ~ ~ ~

On Working Through Pain
and Uncertainty

If there's one thing I've learned, trying to stay in a young person's game through middle age, it's that life is never as simple and straightforward as you think it's going to be. If you really love people and go for big dreams, life is going to be messy. No matter how carefully you plan ahead, no matter how thoroughly you've researched your options, no matter how many times you've practiced your start or told yourself you believe you can win, a lot of what happens is still beyond your control.

As I've said, I'm a type-A person (okay, A++). I put as much energy into beating back the chaos of daily life as anybody I know. The backseat of my car, where Tessa rides, is not filled with Cheerios. The food in my pantry is organized. My books are arranged by height on the shelf. But still I can't control the really important things. My loved ones still get sick. Sometimes they even die. And in my experience, these things often happen at precisely the times when I'm hoping to tune everything out and swim.

Like most swimmers, swimming gives me the feeling—really, the illusion—that life is orderly. The pool is (almost) always 50 meters. The water is (almost) always 79 degrees. The starter always blows a series of short whistles. Then he blows a long whistle. Then he fires the starting signal. There are always eight swimmers in each race. The top-seeded swimmer is in lane four. The length of the race is determined in advance. The person who touches first wins.

But that's not what real life is like. Real life is unpredictable and sometimes even unfair. For that reason, one of the most important skills for a competitive swimmer is the ability to leave whatever's going on in your personal life outside the pool. Some athletes compartmentalize, others vent. There is no one right route. Still, you need to know how to deal with your emotions in order to perform. Because if your emotional house is not in order, it doesn't matter how hard you've trained. Nobody cares how fast you swim on your best day in practice. Swimmers need to swim fast at meets, and those are scheduled long in advance.

In my life, good things and bad things often happen at the same time. My father got really sick and died during the same period of time in which I got pregnant with and gave birth to Tessa. Similarly, the 2008 Olympics were far more rewarding, and far more painful, than I could have guessed.

I didn't see it coming, though maybe I should have. I finished swimming at Trials in Omaha on a Sunday night. The next morning, I flew into San Francisco. Mark Schubert, now the head coach of the Olympic swim team, picked me up at the hotel and drove me down to the Stanford campus for Olympic training camp. That afternoon, I worked out in the weight room. The next morning, Tuesday, I swam early and then caught a plane to Los Angeles to be on *The Tonight Show with Jay Leno*. Leno made me flex my biceps on air, which was really embarrassing. (I made him flex back.)

When my segment was over, I flew immediately back to San Francisco. We had a team meeting that Tuesday night with a special guest speaker. Mark, once again my coach, might have mellowed a bit with age, but he was still strict and intimidating. No way could I miss that meeting.

After Trials in Omaha, Tessa had flown with my mother to Sun Valley. David, her father, flew back home to work. Michael, my coach, flew to Florida, too, where he planned to have surgery on his herniated disc. Seven other swimmers who'd trained with him and me in Coral Springs were heading to the Olympics. (I was the only American.) We all planned to meet up in Singapore, where the U.S. team would hold its second training camp. In the meantime, while Michael and I were separated, we spoke several times a day. He e-mailed me my next day's workout every night. We discussed it before I practiced, and I reported back to him afterward how I felt.

I felt a little funny being a 40-something mother at an Olympic training camp. Camp is really the right word for it. The campers—of which I was one—really have no control over anything. You're told where to sleep, when to sleep, where to eat, when to eat, when to rest, and when to swim. The idea is to give you nothing to worry about, but as a result you feel like a kid. There's even a parents' visiting weekend. Our team included 25 rookies, swimmers who'd never competed at an Olympics before. The youngest was Elizabeth Beisel, who was 15 years old. The girls elected me co-captain, along with Natalie Coughlin and Amanda Beard, but the truth is that most of the younger swimmers didn't know what to make of me, just as in 1984, at my first Olympics, I didn't know what to make of the seemingly ancient Jill Sterkel, who was then 23 years old. Nobody knew that I'd broken down emotionally in the hotel hallway during Olympic Trials. Nobody knew I saw a medium when I needed courage. The other swimmers had only seen me in the warm-up pool and up on the blocks, where I looked confident. But as I knew well, performing is a skill; it's something you practice and learn, just like a start or a stroke. Everyone feels scared inside sometimes. The secret is knowing how to deal with your hard feelings so they don't undermine your hard work.

For the first few days of training camp I mostly hung around with Amanda Beard, who was heading to her fourth Olympic Games. (At her first, in 1996, she'd been only 14 years old and brought her teddy bear with her up onto the medal stand.) I was 15 years older than Amanda, the next-oldest female swimmer on the team, and the only one who was a mom. I didn't ask for special treatment, apart from having my own room. I even signed the same code of conduct I had on my first international trip with the National team, promising to leave my door open if someone of the opposite sex was visiting my room.

Besides feeling old, I mostly felt privileged to be an Olympic athlete again. It's really one of the most amazing honors a person can experience. For a short time you're not just your regular self, living your regular life, swimming with your regular team. You're an athlete representing your country, and that stirs up strong feelings of patriotism, sort of like those I imagine a soldier feels. During that first camp, we all received our official Olympic gear—regular sweats, dress sweats, opening and closing ceremony outfits, practice suits, swim caps, T-shirts, backpacks, even roller bags. (Yes! Roller bags!) We even learned a few words of Chinese.

For me the five weeks between Trials and Games felt like barely enough time, given that I needed to ramp my yardage back up and then taper down again, all while flying halfway around the world. So I just put my head down. I did my workouts and tried to rest. I didn't interact much with the outside world. I talked to David, Tessa, and my mom, and that was pretty much it.

By that point, I was closer to Michael than I'd ever been to a coach. He understood my complicated mix of competitiveness, confidence, and vulnerability. He appreciated my need to control some areas of my life, and my willingness to relinquish control in others. I later learned that after Michael saw me race at the Sette Colli in Rome, my first international meet, he instantly felt that I could medal in the 2008 Olympic Games. He said he'd seen something in me, like a jockey might see in a racehorse—that part of me that was born for speed. From that day forward, Michael trusted my instincts and my talent. Our workouts were hard, but they were never brutal. He understood that I needed to train a whole lot less. Most important, he believed I could win that way.

I don't think I could have trained as successfully with a young coach. I don't think I would have trusted someone less experienced than me. Michael and I had a worn-in, easy rapport, like George Burns and Gracie Allen. At Trials we held a joint press conference. A reporter asked Michael how it was to train me.

"It's a little different, you know, than you would coach an eight-year-old. Dara is a little bit high maintenance."

I punched him in the arm.

But then, about halfway through training camp at Stanford, five days before our team was scheduled to fly to Singapore, Michael called to tell me that he'd gone into the hospital for the pre-op blood work for his hernia surgery, and it turned out he was suffering from something much worse. His herniated disc was the least of his problems. Something was seriously wrong with his blood. His blood work showed almost no red blood cells and very few platelets. Operating was out of the question. Doctors had immediately admitted Michael to try to figure out what was wrong. So far they knew his immune system was severely compromised. He was weak and susceptible to infection. Michael was not even allowed to shave, lest he get a cut. Nobody knew how long he'd live.

I couldn't believe what I was hearing. Could Michael really be facing this? It seemed surreal. I was scared for him. And I have to admit, I was scared for me, too. I'd lost my father less than two years earlier, just as I'd started swimming again. I couldn't bear to lose Michael now.

"Do you have leukemia?" I asked.

Michael said he didn't know.

"What about the C-word? Do you have cancer?"

Michael said he didn't know that either.

His voice sounded awful. I needed to be near him. I told Michael I wanted to leave training camp and fly to Florida, but he refused to allow it.

"Don't worry, honey. I'll be here when you get back." He meant he'd still be alive when I returned from Beijing.

~ ~ ~ ~ ~

Within a few days Michael was diagnosed with a disease called aplastic anemia, a rare blood disorder in which the bone marrow does not produce new blood cells. If left untreated—and nobody knew how long Michael had been untreated, but clearly it had been a while, given how exhausted he'd been for weeks—people die within six months. I called David. He immediately started calling his medical connections. David quickly learned that the best place in the country for Michael to be treated was at the National Heart, Lung, and Blood Institute of the National Institutes of Health, in Bethesda, Maryland. So David called Dr. Neal Young, the leading aplastic anemia expert there, and convinced him to treat Michael. Next, David and friends set about finding transport for Michael from Florida to Maryland. David is like me in a crisis: He needs to do something. It was driving me nuts how helpless I was. My own daughter and her father were not allowed in my hotel room, and my coach was dying, and all I was supposed to do was eat, rest, and swim.

I felt pretty crazy there at camp. Our schedule was designed to be so low-key that many swimmers got bored and started asking the coaches if we could go do something exciting, like play miniature golf. I cried throughout the night after hearing Michael's diagnosis, and I cried all the next morning, particularly when I was supposed to board the van to the Stanford pool. I felt so upset. I couldn't believe this was happening. I needed Michael now, more than ever. And I knew from mourning my father how debilitating grief could be.

Amy Stromwell, our team doctor, knew about the situation with Michael. I'd been hanging out with Amy quite a bit, as she was one of the only people around my age. So instead of taking the team van, she suggested the two of us walk to practice. I sobbed the whole way through lovely Palo Alto, and in the water, as I knew would be the case, my goggles filled up with tears. I seemed able to pull myself together only for short spurts, a few hundred meters at a time. Then I'd hang on the gutter and cry again. Meanwhile, my teammates streamed by, heads down, arms clapping the surface of the water, their thoughts where they should be: Beijing.

Mark Schubert, the coach who always seemed to pop up in my life just when I needed him, was leading my practices. He conferred with Michael every day—the two were old friends and had coached together at Mission Bay in Florida in the 1980s—but the truth is that Michael was pretty out of it. The day before we left for Singapore, Michael was transferred from Florida to the National Institutes of Health. I called him there shortly before I left the country.

"How are you doing, Michael?" I asked. I really wanted to know the truth.

"It's pretty bad," he said. "I think I deal with these things pretty well, but this is hard."

I started crying uncontrollably, as I'd been doing for days. "You promised me you'd be here when I got back."

Michael started backpedaling on that promise. "Yeah, I know. I'm fighting with everything I can."

~ ~ ~ ~ ~

In Maryland, doctors put Michael on an immunosuppressant treatment called ATG. They believed the T-cells in Michael's blood were attacking his bone marrow, so for four days they pumped his body with high doses of a drug that attacks T-cells. The hope was that this would enable Michael's bone marrow to produce blood cells again. But the ATG treatment had serious side effects. The first day of Michael's scheduled four-day therapy his temperature spiked to 104 degrees. He landed in the ICU and remembers nothing from that day. The next day Michael's temperature started coming down, but he developed a wheezing in his chest that scared everybody.

The last night of Trials, after the 50-meter freestyle finals, Michael and I had decided, together with Mark Schubert, that I wasn't going to swim the individual 100-meter freestyle in Beijing. The three extra heats at that distance—preliminaries, semifinals, and finals—would put too much strain on my body, particularly my shoulder, and probably damage my chances of winning a gold medal in the 50-meter freestyle, where I had the best shot. Most of the time I was okay with this decision, but sometimes I had doubts. I'd worked so hard to get to the Olympics, and now I was going to back out of a race?

One day, as I was wavering on whether scratching the individual 100-meter freestyle had been the right decision, Bernard called my cell phone to wish me luck. "You're making the right decision," he assured me, even though I hadn't yet told him what was on my mind and there's no way he could have known that I'd chosen to let the individual 100-meter freestyle go.

But Michael was adamant that I should still anchor the 4 × 100-meter freestyle relay and the 4 × 100-meter medley relay. I'd earned both positions by winning the 100-meter freestyle at Olympic Trials. Even as Michael lay in the National Institutes of Health, fighting for his life, he was arguing with Mark Schubert and the other Olympic team coaches for me to keep that spot.

"If you want to do justice to Dara, you'll put her last," he said to anybody who would listen.

He was making these calls from his hospital nightie. How could they say no?

I could anchor both events swimming only in the finals, as rules allow teams to use alternates in the preliminaries relays, and there are no semifinals in relay events. My main concern was that the finals of the medley relay were to be only 30 minutes after the finals of the 50-meter freestyle. That was barely enough time to warm down, get stretched, and return to the ready room. But Mark and Michael both felt confident I could make the transition, so I tried to feel confident, too.

Apart from vivid memories of thinking and worrying about Michael, most of the five weeks between Trials and the Games is a blur. I tried to keep up my routine from Coral Springs as best I could. Every day I drank a Living Fuel shake for breakfast, plus one scoop of amino acids. After my workout I had five more scoops of amino acids, to aid my muscle recovery, and another four scoops of aminos each night before bed. I consumed no coffee and no alcohol. I slept nine hours a night. My stretchers, Anne and Steve, had flown with me to Palo Alto, and then Singapore, too. So far my shoulder was holding up, but this wasn't the time for me to stop getting massaged, aligned, and stretched.

One of the traditions of the Olympic swim team is rookie skits. This is just what it sounds like—groups of four or five first-time Olympians get up there in front of everybody and make total goofballs of themselves. If you've only ever seen Olympic swimmers on TV, you might think we're an intimidating bunch. But a lot of swimmers are sort of clumsy on land (perhaps due to the hyperflexible ankles). Plus, most of us have spent our prime years, when we should have been gaining experience and maturity, swatting each other with towels and staring at black lines in pools.

A few of the rookies tried to argue that, technically, I was a rookie again. They had some theory about statutes of limitations, that if you miss an Olympics you forfeit your veteran status. But . . . no, that wasn't happening. One rookie skit was enough for me, thank you very much. Still, that didn't protect me from getting thoroughly roasted. As we sat in our hotel in Singapore, where the exchange rate was so crazy iced tea cost $25, one group of rookie swimmers after another got up with someone impersonating me, wheeling around a roller bag, hair pushed straight up in a headband (that's how I wear mine when I'm not in the water or dressed up), commanding her groupies to mash her with their feet, feed her peeled grapes, and wipe sweat off her brow. It was pretty funny, and I definitely felt busted. I could see how, from the kids' perspective, flying Anne and Steve halfway around the world looked like megalomaniacal rock-star behavior. But the truth is that they weren't there for my ego. Anne and Steve were part of my commitment to excellence, to being flawlessly prepared.

Back at the National Institutes of Health, Michael was recovering from the fever brought on by his ATG treatment. But by that point, doctors were worrying even more about a second disease. In addition to failing to produce new blood cells due to aplastic anemia, Michael's body was attacking the platelets he was getting through blood transfusions. Doctors would give Michael a transfusion of whole blood but all the platelets in that blood would disappear quickly. Platelets are important to the body because they cause blood to clot when you get a cut on your skin or bleed inside. Most adults have platelet counts of between 150,000 and 450,000 units per microliter of blood. Michael's platelet count was 7,000 units per microliter of blood. Any nick or cut was life-threatening. So along with his other problems—his herniated disc, his lack of energy, his risk of infection—Michael could now bleed to death. Michael's wife, Biggi, sent me a picture. Michael looked like he was growing a Santa beard.

I still talked to Michael every day. He tried to play down his problems for me, but his prognosis was unclear. No one knew how well his aplastic anemia would respond to the ATG treatment. No one knew how to control his platelet situation. And he still had debilitating pain in his back.

Ten days before the start of the Olympics, I was so sapped by worrying about Michael, and worrying that my preoccupation with him was going to affect my swimming, that I went to talk to the team psychologist, Jim Bauman. Finishing my workouts was difficult for me. I wasn't cheerful at the pool. So Jim came to my hotel room and asked what I was most distressed about. I told him that I was most distressed that Michael was going to die when I was at the Olympics. Jim asked me to put my distress level on a scale of one to ten, I put it at eight or nine. Jim then asked me about my fears, or as he called them, my "negative belief systems." I told him I felt like everything was out of my control. Next Jim reformulated this into a positive belief: "I have control over some things in my life but not others." He asked me how much I believed this statement. On a scale of one to seven, I put my belief at a one.

Given the Games began in less than two weeks, I didn't have time to work through all my issues in traditional talk therapy, so Jim had me do a technique called eye movement designation reprocessing, which replicates the way your brain processes information during the rapid eye movement, or REM, phase of sleep. Psychologists use it to help process trauma in assault or accident victims and military vets. The idea behind it is that bad thoughts can get stuck in our working memories. We sometimes need help filing them away. If you can't get bad thoughts out of your working memory, you feel traumatized. These thoughts spring to the forefront of your mind too frequently and at inappropriate times.

For 90 minutes, during my first session with Jim, he moved two fingers across my field of vision, left to right, right to left. I kept my head still and followed his fingers with my eyes, mimicking the eye movement in REM sleep. First Jim told me to conjure up the most disturbing situation I could imagine, and I pictured Michael in a hospital bed with tubes hanging out all over his body and me in Beijing not realizing how sick he really was. As I described this picture to Jim, he kept moving his fingers in front of my eyes. I cried torrentially, as I had in my father's mausoleum. Every 10 minutes, Jim would pause and ask me what was at the forefront of my mind.

"I still imagine Michael in bed, in pain," I said.

"Okay, let's go with that," Jim said. We'd talk about that for a while longer, Jim still moving his fingers, me still following them with my eyes.

A few minutes later, he'd ask again. "Okay, what's in your working memory now?"

"I'm so far away, I can't be there for him."

The point of our session was not to get to the bottom of all my feelings. The point was to help my brain find a way to store my bad thoughts so I could concentrate on my swimming without feeling distracted and obsessed. After an hour and a half of talking, crying, and following Jim's fingers with my eyes, Jim asked me to put numbers on his distress and belief scales again. This time, when he asked me how distressed I felt when I imagined Michael in the hospital and myself in Beijing, I said, "That's more like a two."

When he asked how truthful it seemed that we could have control over some things in life but not in others, I put my belief at five or six.

Jim and I did another session the next day, trying further to clear my working memory from obsessive, traumatic thoughts. Afterward, I felt much better—not done worrying about Michael but better able to control my thinking about him.

The day we were scheduled to fly to China I woke up very early, packed, and hit the hotel gym at 5:00 A.M. so I could work out before we left for the airport at 6:15 A.M. I was the only one of my teammates in the weight room. When I finished, I showered, dressed, and called Michael again.

"You go out there and finish the story we started together," Michael told me.

To do that, I'd need to excel under pressure.

I slept on the flight to Beijing.

11

~ ~ ~ ~ ~

On Growing as an Athlete

One of the things I love most about swimming is that it's constantly teaching me something new. My races are just a length or two in a water-filled rectangle. After racing in pools for 34 years, what could be left to learn? Yet even in that circumscribed world, I continue to be surprised. It's sort of like listening to a favorite song every four or eight years. The most interesting part is how it sounds different. In those differences you can see how you've changed.

That's how Beijing was for me. It was my fifth Olympics. You'd think it might be old hat. But nothing could have been further from the truth. Those Olympics were exhilarating, and despite all the energy I'd put into establishing routines, they were unpredictable, too. In Beijing I found myself doing things and feeling things I never expected to do or feel. Waiting again in those ready rooms, where swimmers are supposed to collect their nerves and energy before a race, standing up on those blocks, I felt so much more comfortable in myself than I ever had before. Since I'd last competed in an Olympics, my father had died and Tessa had been born. Late though it may have been, I'd finally become an adult—if your definition of an adult is someone who's truly learned to live both within and outside of themselves—and that became clear to me in unexpected ways.

I knew from the moment I arrived in Beijing that I was different, or these Olympics were different, because for the first time I was not disappointed. The reality of being there matched or surpassed the fantasy I'd been carrying around in my head. I know some people (like my mother) have different opinions on this, but I loved Beijing. I loved the Olympic Village. I loved the landscaping. I loved my dorm room. I loved my bed. I loved my pillow. I even loved my crisp white cotton sheets.

I also loved the Water Cube, with its bubble-like, sun-filled membranes—it was so light and airy inside (or, I should say, it was so light and airy after the first day, when the smog trapped on the ceiling had cleared). I loved the competition pool, with its wide ten lanes. I loved the showers. I even loved the mixed zone, where reporters shouted questions at you. Perhaps most surprising, given how nauseous I always get with anxiety, I loved the crazy intensity of the Games themselves. I couldn't wait to get out there and race. I felt acutely aware of what a privilege it all was. I felt that deep, appreciative, happy-to-be-there enthusiasm of a woman who was supposed to have hung up her Speedo many years before.

My first race, the 4 × 100-meter freestyle relay, went off without much drama, which was just fine with me. Swimming fast is the natural result of being fully prepared. It's not meant to be theatrical. It's simply the reward for setting up difficult tasks, then achieving them day in and day out. I'd arrived in China with the team on August 4, five days before my first swim. During that downtime I focused almost entirely on establishing my routine—on getting used to the pools and life in the Olympic Village, and working out all the times I needed to do everything in reverse. Each day, I planned my schedule backward from the moment when I wanted to dive in the pool. If I was to start swimming at 10:00 A.M., what time would I need to clear security at the Water Cube? And to clear security at that time, what time would I need to arrive at the Water Cube door? And to arrive at the Water Cube door at that time, what bus would I need to catch from the Olympic Village?

Rowdy Gaines, when he swam in the 1984 Olympics, studied the starter before his race to see how quickly he tended to pull the gun. Anybody *could* have done that, but Rowdy actually did it. As a result, he had an excellent start. I was trying to follow the same philosophy. As Mark Schubert had first taught me at Mission Viejo, you have to care about every detail, every day, if you want to win.

My goal was to keep my training schedule as similar as possible to a day in Coral Springs, and my prerace schedule similar to the one I'd established at the Sette Colli in Rome. So in the days leading up to that freestyle relay, I didn't worry about scouting the competition. I just focused on my swimming and on keeping my mind and body relaxed. Each morning, as I had for the previous two years, I drank my Living Fuel shake for breakfast. Then I took the bus over to the Water Cube and swam between 1,100 and 3,000 meters (depending on how many days it was until my next race. I swam fewer meters if my race was sooner). After that, Anne and Steve mashed me and stretched me out. Then I returned to my dorm room to rest.

Waiting to race in the Olympics is a peculiar experience. As Dawn Fraser, who won the 100-meter freestyle in the 1956, 1960, and 1964 Olympics and who was the first woman to break a minute in that event, described it in her book *Below the Surface: Confessions of an Olympic Champion,* "On the day of an Olympic final you feel like something delicate—a wedding cake, maybe, or a spring hat—that shouldn't be touched. You lie around on your back for most of the day, and you feel that the blanket around you should be cotton wool or even tissue paper. The other athletes leave you alone a lot, unless you say you want to talk. The atmosphere is hushed and the care is special, as if you're in a hospital ward. Because their fitness is so vital, Olympic athletes suffer from occupational hypochondria. They always feel that something is going to go wrong—that their muscles will seize up or that they'll cave in with a chill. On that last day, when you know you have the ability to do well, you don't want to take a single risk. You walk slowly to the mess hall and you eat things that can't possibly affect your tummy. . . . You have an important appointment that night, possibly with a gold medal, and it dances in the mist of your mind all the time. You can talk about other things, but you can't stop thinking about the moment to come on the starting block."

That's how I felt. I sort of couldn't believe that this was happening, that the moment I'd been working toward so methodically for so long had arrived. Apart from Michael's getting sick, everything had gone according to plan. In the preliminaries of the 4 × 100-meter freestyle relay two young swimmers, Emily Silver and Julia Smit, swam for Natalie Coughlin and me so that we could keep our bodies rested for our upcoming events. (I was swimming in three events. Natalie was swimming in six.) On the morning of the finals, I woke up early and went down to the team room to read my overflowing e-mail inbox, which I now found energizing instead of stressful. At the Water Cube, I did my wake-up swim, my mashing session, my warm-up swim, my hot shower, and my stretching session. Then I put on the bottom half of my racing suit and headed to the ready room.

Our freestyle relay team consisted of Natalie Coughlin, Lacey Nymeyer, Kara Lynn Joyce, and me. We all rode a huge wave of adrenaline as we walked out to the pool deck. Speedo, along with the fashion house Comme des Garçons, had designed for us the most incredible star-studded red-white-and-blue LZR racing suits. As we were pulling off our sweat clothes and stashing them in our bin, I noticed President George Bush, down low in the stands, waving an American flag at us.

"Hey, guys," I said to my teammates, "President Bush is waving at us!"

Who's too old to love that?

Natalie swam our leadoff leg. I cheered my lungs out for her, just as I did for Lacey and Kara. I was swimming last. Before I dove in, I told myself one thing and one thing only (I can't seem to remember more than that in a race): Don't look for the other swimmers until you touch. Near the end of the 2000 Olympics in Sydney, my coach, Richard Quick, who was also one of the coaches for the Olympic team, showed the entire Olympic team a video of me swimming in the finals of the 4 × 100-meter free-style relay. I'd practically stopped in the middle and lifted my head up like a baby seal to see how I was doing relative to the other swimmers. "This is what I'd better NOT see you do," Richard announced to the team, making a teaching moment of my gaffe. My relay team had won gold that day, but that was not the point. I was not going to lift my head up in a race again.

Natalie got off to a good start. On the first of her two lengths of the pool she was on world-record pace. Britta Steffen, of Germany, passed her, but that didn't concern me, because I knew the rest of the German girls were not as strong as Britta. But Natalie had a tough second 50 meters. When she touched the wall and Lacey, our second swimmer, dove in, we were behind Germany and Great Britain, in third place. Lacey swam well, too, and maintained the third-place spot behind Germany and the Netherlands, whose team was quickly gaining ground. Still, Kara, our third swimmer, and I had nearly impossible jobs ahead of us if we were to win. We knew the Germans would fade, but we also knew that the Dutch would not, and that the Australians could come on strong in the final two legs. The Dutch had a very deep team, the same four women who had just smashed the world record at the European Championships in March. Swimming against me in the anchor leg would be Dutchwoman Marleen Velduis, who had the fastest relay split in the 100-meter freestyle in history, and Australian Libby Trickett, who held the world record in the individual 100-meter freestyle.

Kara gained on the Germans and came back to the wall in second place, trailing the Dutch by less than a second. I kept my head down and made up some ground against Marleen, but on the back half I ran out of room. When I finished, I didn't know if I'd held off Libby or how fast I'd swum. Looking up at the scoreboard, I learned that we'd won silver. I'd swum fast enough to hold off Libby Trickett and force the Australians to take bronze.

So that was it: my tenth Olympic medal! Sure, I would have preferred gold, but I felt great. I swam under the lane line and hugged Marleen, the Dutch swimmer. Then I noticed Mark Schubert, in the stands, flashing his fingers at me. First five fingers, then two fingers, then four fingers.

I shrugged, not understanding what he was trying to tell me. So he did it again.

First five fingers, then two fingers, then four fingers.

Then I got it: I'd swum my split in 52.4 seconds! That was the second-fastest 100-meter relay split by a woman in history. It was also almost a full second faster than my previous personal best. I'd beaten the "5" "4" "." "8" I'd had manicured on my fingernails in 1984 by more than two seconds. If nothing else happened at these Olympic Games, I'd still go home triumphant. I'd proven to the world that you *can* get faster as you get older. I was a flesh-and-blood example that an athlete can achieve as much in her forties as she did in her teens and twenties.

~ ~ ~ ~ ~

After the freestyle relay, I had five days to rest before my individual 50-meter race. At the beginning of that window, I showed my family around the Olympic Village. I indulged myself in a few Olympic perks, like hanging out with basketball players Kobe Bryant and Jason Kidd, and eating with the hunky guys on the American men's water polo team. But mostly I just took it easy and stuck to my routine. Each day I swam, rested, got mashed and stretched, and watched my teammates compete. This, of course, meant watching Michael Phelps rack up his eight gold medals. I rarely got too nervous for Michael. He's so consistent and such a natural-born swimming machine. Even though he still called me "Mom," I looked up to him in some ways. He's masterful at performing under pressure. On the morning of my semifinals in the 50-meter freestyle, I watched him as he was vying for his seventh gold medal, this time in the 100-meter butterfly.

By the time Michael stepped on deck, I'd almost finished preparing. I'd done my wake-up swim, my warm-up swim, and my body-work. I'd raised my core temperature. I even put on the bottom half of my racing suit. Of course, I was a little bit queasy, but I felt confident I'd be among the 8 out of 16 semifinal swimmers to move forward into the finals. I just needed to stay focused. I knew I'd worked harder than any other swimmer in the Water Cube. I felt a gold medal in the 50-meter freestyle was mine to lose.

During Michael Phelps's 100-meter butterfly race, I stood on the edge of the team area with my iPod cranked up. I wanted to see him perform, but I also didn't want my energies pulled too far outside myself. At the start Milorad Čavić, of Serbia, took an early lead and halfway through the race Michael was still behind. *Oh, my gosh, he's actually going to lose,* I remember thinking. But on the back 50 meters Michael dug down deep. Both he and Čavić appeared to reach the wall at exactly the same time. The entire Water Cube stared up at the scoreboard, as nobody could tell who had won with the naked eye. According to the official clock, Michael had beat Čavić by one one-hundredth of a second, the smallest possible margin in Olympic swimming.

One one-hundredth of a second? I couldn't really believe it. I'd won hundreds of races and lost hundreds of races, and even tied with Jenny for a bronze in the 100-meter freestyle in the 2000 Olympic Games, but I'd never been out-touched by such a narrow margin. *Oh, my God, that poor guy!* I thought to myself. But I didn't have time to dwell on it. I needed to clear my head of all distractions and report to the ready room for my own race.

Because the 50-meter freestyle is just one length of the pool, the race starts at the opposite end from all the other events, so the finish is in the same place. Typically, aquatic centers have just one ready room, but the Water Cube had two, a main one close to where most races start and a second, at the other end of the arena, specifically for 50-meter races. I didn't want to sit in either of these rooms. Ready rooms just make me tense. Two-time Olympian Amy van Dyken, when asked how she liked the ready room, once replied, "You mean the white-padded room?" Don Schollander, another American swimming legend, was notorious for playing ready-room head games. "Psyching out is part of the game. You've got to be able to take it and you've got to be able to do it," he wrote in his memoir, *Deep Water.* Proving his point, at the 1964 Olympic Games, in the ready room before the men's 100-meter freestyle, Schollander kept sliding along a bench, inching ever closer to the Frenchman Alain Gottvalles, who'd vowed he could beat Schollander after smoking half a pack of cigarettes and drinking a bottle of wine. Eventually, Gottvalles got fed up with Schollander's sliding and walked into the bathroom. Schollander followed and stood behind him at the urinal.

A few minutes later, Schollander won gold. Gottvalles came in fifth.

On the morning of my semifinal, after handing over my credentials at the main ready room, I walked down a long hall, past a bunch of Speedo representatives, to the 50-meter-only ready room near the far end of the pool. My shoulder had started hurting a little bit, but my plan was just to swim through the pain. I knew a couple of the other swimmers in the semifinal heats: Kara Lynn Joyce, who'd swum with me on the 4 × 100-meter freestyle relay; Arlene Semeco, from Venezuela, who'd trained with me in Coral Springs; and Therese Alshammar, from Sweden, who'd beat me in the 50-meter freestyle in the 2000 Olympic Games. (She won silver; I took bronze.) Like me, Therese was a 50-meter specialist. She, too, had scratched her spot in the individual 100-meter freestyle so she could focus on winning the event. Along with Britta Steffen of Germany and Libby Trickett of Australia, Therese was one of my primary threats. I'd never beat Therese in the long-course 50-meter freestyle. Her personal-best time in the event was 24.23 seconds. Mine was 24.25 seconds.

Therese, Arlene, and I had berths in the second semifinal heat; Britta and Kara were in the first. Both groups left that second ready room together and sat for a few minutes in those hidden rows of chairs under the stands. According to the schedule, the first and second semifinal heats were separated by only a few minutes. While we waited for the first group to finish up, Cate Campbell, a 16-year-old from Australia, and I tried to sneak around the corner, hoping to see who'd won. We inched out as far as we could without becoming visible, yet we never caught a glimpse of the scoreboard. By that point, it was time for us to get organized anyway. We walked back to our chairs to put on our caps and collect our goggles in order to walk out on deck.

Then, just as I was pushing my hair under my cap, I felt a tap on my shoulder. It was Therese.

Her cap was already in place. She was wearing only her racing suit and her sweat bottoms. She looked really scared.

Without saying anything, she turned around.

Her suit had split open along the zipper all the way down her back. The latch of her zipper was stuck up near her shoulder blades. Beneath was a gaping oval the length of her spine.

"Can you help me?" she asked.

I didn't give it a second thought or even really answer her. I just got to work, trying to force the slider back down so I could pull it up again, this time with the teeth engaged. I couldn't really believe this was happening to her. I'd panicked so badly when my own suit had ripped at the rinky-dink Missouri Grand Prix. Now here was Therese, just moments before the Olympic semifinals. If she scratched this heat, there'd be no finals for her. I didn't feel like her competitor anymore. I felt like a mother about to watch her daughter miss out on her dream.

The rest of the girls either didn't see what had happened or were too focused on their upcoming swim to take in the situation. So I enlisted help from the Swedish official who happened to be our chaperone. He held together the sides of Therese's zipper while I did my best to wiggle down the latch.

Every few moments, the thought would flit through my head: *I shouldn't be doing this. What if my hands cramp up?* Just putting on a suit in the best of circumstances can cause your hand muscles to flood with lactic acid. I'd bought a squeeze ball to build up strength in my own hands to ensure that I didn't develop cramps just putting on my suit. Therese's situation was clearly going to be cramp inducing, but I couldn't worry about that. She needed help. What's more, I *wanted* to help her. I'd come here to race against the best in the world. I wanted Therese swimming in the semifinal, even if she beat me in the end.

Finally, I worked Therese's slider down to a couple of inches from the zipper's bottom. Then it stuck for good. By this point, the Olympic organizers had cued the music signaling it was time for the next heat of swimmers to walk out on deck. At a normal swim meet, cued marching music would not have been that big a deal. But at the Olympics, hundreds of people in dozens of countries sign off on those schedules, including many broadcasters like NBC. When the officials cue the marching music, you march.

So I pulled up Therese's zipper from that point. She still had a small hole in her suit where the zipper teeth were not engaged near the base of her spine. But the fabric seemed to be staying closed, and I didn't think the suit would fill up with water like a water balloon. "Whatever you do, don't bend down until you need to start," I told Therese.

I bent over to grab my goggles off my chair. Therese squatted to pick up hers.

That's when I heard that awful synthetic rip.

By that point, the marching music had been playing for 20 seconds. I walked out on deck. Therese did not. Behind me I heard running and yelling, presumably Therese and the Swedish official heading toward the Speedo representatives halfway down that long hall to get her a new suit. How she could get a new suit on in time was sort of hard to imagine—putting on a LZR suit takes many swimmers upward of 20 minutes—but I didn't know what to do except proceed. On deck, I took off the two T-shirts I was wearing and used them to dry my block. Then I walked over to the side of the pool to splash water on my arms and face.

I hated that Therese was going to have to scratch this race

because of a broken zipper. That's not the vision I have of my sport. So I decided to tell the deck officials about Therese's suit. I'd never heard of an Olympic race being delayed, but I had nothing to lose. As nonchalantly as I could, I walked over to Carol Zaleski, a woman I knew from her job as a past president of USA Swimming, who happened to be one of the deck officials for our race.

"Excuse me, Carol, one of the girls in our heat, her suit ripped."

Carol looked really surprised that I was talking to her, but also receptive, so I kept talking. "Therese isn't out. I think she's trying to change her suit. Is there any way you can hold the heat?"

Carol said, "We'll delay the start as long as we can."

I walked back to my block. I still didn't have a plan. I was just going on instinct. Never in my 34 years of competitive swimming had I talked with anyone on deck right before a race, but Arlene, Cate, and the other girls already had their goggles over their eyes. They were shaking out their arms, psyching up their bodies to dive in within 30 seconds. They needed to know Therese wasn't out and Carol was hoping to delay the start.

"Hey, you guys," I said to anyone who understood English. "Therese isn't out yet. Her suit ripped. This might be a few minutes. We all just need to relax." For the non–English speakers I made a gesture like a schoolteacher. I put my hands out flat in front of me and patted the air, like I was telling a class to settle down.

I knew this wasn't ideal, especially for the younger swimmers who were almost certainly growing tenser by the minute instead of better prepared. But we didn't have a choice. Nobody plans on a broken zipper. I think it's safe to say every swimmer on deck would have wanted the same courtesy extended to her had she been in Therese's suit.

So we all paced, breathed, and flapped our arms for a few more moments. Then Therese came running out.

How she got that suit on so fast I still don't know. I haven't had the chance to ask her, as I haven't seen her since. The officials gave Therese a couple of seconds to gather her composure. Then we mounted our blocks and listened for the starting signal.

Over the years, I've become very adept at snapping in and out of focus, so even after all that chaos I felt prepared. For this Olympics I'd had my toenails painted with American flags, and as I curled them over the edge of the block I felt a wave of calm wash over me. I'd come into Beijing promoted almost solely as a feel-good story. Not even my old friend Rowdy Gaines, who was doing live television commentary for NBC, thought I was a serious contender for the gold medal. He just thought my story was catchy because of my age. I breathed in and prepared myself to react to the starting signal. When I reached the wall, once again I had no idea how fast I'd swum.

This time when I looked up at the scoreboard I saw that I'd touched in 24.27 seconds, only .02 off my personal best. I felt great—just where I wanted to be. I'd won the semifinals. No one could doubt any longer that I had a real shot at the gold.

After the race, as I was warming down, trying to flush some of that lactic acid out of my muscles before tomorrow's final, Mark Schubert came running over. "Dara!" he screamed, just like he used to when I was a kid. "I didn't know what the hell you were doing! I kept thinking, *Oh, my God, is something wrong?* You almost gave me a heart attack! But you looked more relaxed helping Therese than I've ever seen you look before the start of any race."

I'd felt more relaxed, too—and I'll tell you why: my age.

~ ~ ~ ~ ~

That night, at the Olympic Village, I ate a light early dinner and retreated to my room. The next day was the last day of swimming competition. I'd be swimming in the finals of the 50-meter free-style and also anchoring the 4 × 100-meter medley relay. But it was in the 50-meter freestyle that I was either going to fail or attain my goal.

I felt strange being there alone in the Olympic Village. I really missed Tessa, and I really missed Michael, yet here I was, by myself, psyching up for an Olympic final alone, as I'd done so many times before. I had nothing left to do to prepare for my swim. My only task for the night was to sleep. I'd already called Tessa, who'd screamed into the phone, "Mommy! Mommy, you swim fast!"

To relax I watched a few episodes of the TV series *House,* and as I often do when I'm watching TV, I filed and buffed my nails. I tell you that now because later that little moment of personal hygiene took on outsized importance. Then, shortly before I turned out my light, I called Michael at the National Institutes of Health.

The gruff German who liked to call me "diva" took a whole lot longer to deliver Tessa's same basic "swim fast" advice. Michael sounded weak and very far away. Still, he insisted on recapping for me all the lessons he'd tried to teach me over the past 18 months. Keep my body straight and tight on my start. Rotate my shoulders so I'd have a longer reach on my touch. Don't stop kicking until I'd reached the wall.

I knew all this, and Michael knew I knew it, but we couldn't help ourselves. We needed to go over the game plan one more time.

In the morning, my alarm went off at 6:00 A.M. My race didn't start for four hours and I felt a little groggy, but I didn't want to be rushed. Just as I had before the semifinals, I drank my Living Fuel breakfast shake. I packed and repacked my roller bag—two practice suits, two racing suits, two caps, two pairs of goggles, my warm-up sweats, my dress sweats, my iPod. Then I went downstairs to the team room, where we had an Internet connection, to read some e-mails for inspiration before my race. In just the past 24 hours, more than 75 people had written to me, some of whom I hadn't heard from since high school. Many shared stories about the amazing comebacks they were making in their own lives.

Reading those e-mails gave me that adrenaline surge I normally feel before relays, and it was amplified times ten. For the first time in my life before an individual event, I was not just going out there to swim for myself. I was going out there to swim for everybody who wanted to debunk the conventional wisdom about athletic performance and age. That morning, I came to understand how big dreams work: how they start small, in a single person, but once they take hold, they grow so much larger and so much more powerful than anyone could have guessed.

I must have read 50 or 60 messages that morning. Each message gave me a boost. But one meant more to me than all the rest. It was from Michael. He'd sent it in the middle of the night. "Forget everything I said," he'd written. "Just do your own thing."

~ ~ ~ ~ ~

Everything about that day was normal and surreal. As I told you at the beginning of this book, I took the 6:45 A.M. bus over to the Water Cube. The only other riders were my childhood coach, Mark Schubert, and serendipitously Therese's Swedish coach, who thanked me for my poise in helping Therese with her suit. At the Water Cube, I handed my water bottle over to Mark; I get nervous leaving it unattended at big meets. Then I shouted "Good morning!" to Bob Costas, who was broadcasting from up in the rafters, walked over to the competition pool, found my lane, and dove in. I had that great luxurious feeling of diving into a million gallons of unruffled water all by myself. The water felt so calm and peaceful, like those evenings at Stanford when I'd scaled the fence. Mark stood along the gutter watching my stroke. Meanwhile, I stared down at the bottom of the pool, committing to memory the placement of each underwater camera and intake jet. I wanted to memorize all the landmarks so I could gauge where I'd be each stroke of the race.

In many ways, my whole life had been funneling toward this moment. I'd retired from swimming and come back, and retired from swimming and come back, and retired from swimming and come back again, and now here I was, at age 41, in a better position to win a gold medal in an individual event at the Olympics than I'd ever been before. I had no regrets about my preparation. Even Mark Schubert's stepping in to fill Michael's shoes felt nearly preordained. That morning, after my wake-up swim, I took a hot shower, Anne and Steve mashed me with their feet, I did my warm-up swim, took another hot shower, then Anne and Steve stretched me in a hallway. Finally, it was time to go put on my racing suit. I headed over to the single unisex bathroom where I'd been changing, opened the door, and—I'm sorry, I know this is really gross, but it's just what the Olympics are like—I found some poor guy sitting on the toilet, relieving himself. He was just some college-aged kid, distracted by the heady venue, and he'd forgotten to lock the door. I excused myself and waited outside as long as I could stand it. But after about five minutes I couldn't wait any longer. "Are you going to be long?" I yelled through the door. "I have to get on my suit before my final."

I know, it was rude, but I had a schedule I wanted to stick to.

"Oh, no, no, I'm done now," the guy called back. So I apologized for being so forward and barged in.

"Okay," I said while he was washing his hands. "I have a long T-shirt that's going to cover me while I change. Sorry if you see anything." Then I pulled off my sweats and sat down on the floor. "Please just shut the door when you're done."

Suited up, however immodestly, I put on my iPod and walked over to the team area. There, near the warm-up pool, I sat on a massage table and watched table tennis on TV until one of the coaches told me it was time to report to the ready room. If you don't report to the ready room 15 minutes before your swim, you get disqualified. An American Secret Service agent actually followed me there. I sat down inside. The air felt stale and terrible. I'm not sure what came over me, but I started cracking jokes.

"Anybody else hot? Or is it just me?" I said to Kara Lynn Joyce, my American teammate, Libby Trickett, the Australian world-record holder, and Cate Campbell, the 16-year-old Australian girl who had been in my semifinal heat. The air wasn't circulating very well. "I feel like I'm in menopause."

Everybody started laughing. This was not the standard ready-room talk.

"No, it is kind of hot," Kara reassured me.

"Oh, okay. Thank God," I said.

I wasn't trying to psych anybody out. I just wanted to lighten the mood and have a little fun. I'd spent so much of my swimming life racked with panic, but now that I was here at this bonus Olympics I wanted to enjoy it. Jason Kidd and LeBron James were out there in the Water Cube. There was nowhere I'd rather be.

At the blocks, of course, I pulled my energy inward. I took off my sweats and dried my block with a towel. I walked over to the side of the pool where I'd intercepted the deck official during Therese's suit fiasco and splashed water on my hands and face. I was swimming in lane four, the lane reserved for the top seed. Britta Steffen, of Germany, who'd won the 100-meter freestyle two days before, was seeded third and swimming next to me in lane three. My family and friends were spread throughout the stadium.

I didn't have time to pick out their faces, but I felt their presence and support as I scrambled to finish my prerace routine before the announcer called my name. I dragged the skin of my forearms against the rough surface of the starting block. I checked my goggles and cap. When the loudspeaker called "Dara Torres," I smiled and waved. I was so happy to be here. Just two and a half years earlier, I'd been a pregnant retired swimmer. I mounted my block and gripped its front edge. I rocked my body weight back. At the starting signal, *tone* was the only word in my mind.

Sprinting is an out-of-body experience—all action, little awareness. When I arrived at the far wall, I had no idea who'd won. From the stands, I'm told, I appeared to have led for the first 48 meters, but the experience in the water is different from the experience in the stands. If the race is close, you don't recognize yourself either winning or losing. You just feel yourself moving, like a bullet that's left the gun. So it was only when I reached the wall and I looked up at the scoreboard that I knew I'd come in second. I'd touched in 24.07 seconds, the fastest I'd ever swum by nearly two tenths. I didn't win, but I set a new American record. Just as important, I upended the notion that a swimming career must end at age 25 or 35 or even 40 years old.

In the prior two years, I'd faced so many doubters: Michael, who wouldn't coach me when I first arrived at Coral Springs; the British coach at the Sette Colli meet in Rome who'd laughed at me for being older than one of his swimmers' moms. But now I'd proven to the world that maturity, experience, dedication, and ingenuity can make up for a little senescence. Muscle tightening is not the only thing that happens in our bodies over time. We gain knowledge, focus, and understanding, and those things can help us win.

Unfortunately, my brain then processed the fine points of the information up on that scoreboard: Britta Steffen, of Germany, had touched in 24.06 seconds. She'd beaten me by one one-hundredth of a second. By the narrowest margin in my sport, I'd missed winning gold.

I suppose someone could choose to see this as karmic retribution, payback for all those days when I insisted on beating my brothers at foosball, or my friend Tommie at golf, or David when we rode our bikes. But I'm not inclined to think so. I lost by one one-hundredth of a second—a very small amount of time, but a measurable span nonetheless. I felt proud for having succeeded in just about every set of terms you can define: I'd made the Olympic team, I'd made the finals, I'd broken my own personal record, I'd smashed the American record, and I'd proven that success in athletics at the highest level is possible in middle age. Yet I'd lost, and I hate losing. I swam under the lane line and gave Britta a hug. Then, back in my own lane, I tilted my head against the wall and I allowed myself a small scream.

12

~ ~ ~ ~ ~

On Not Giving Up

I am who I am—a competitor at heart. That hundredth of a second doesn't gnaw at me a little; it gnaws at me a lot. I've heard people say it puts the focus of my comeback in the right place, on blowing open the possibilities as we age. But that's not how I think. I've wanted to win, at everything, every day, since I was a kid. And time doesn't change a person. It just helps you get a handle on who you are. Even at age 41, I still hate losing; I'm just more gracious about it. I'm also aware that setbacks have an upside: They fuel new dreams.

So it was probably fortunate that at the Water Cube I didn't have time to dwell on that hundredth of a second. My next race was too soon. In less than 30 minutes from my touch in the 50-meter freestyle, I needed to warm down, take part in the medal ceremony, pose for pictures with Britta Steffen and Cate Campbell (who'd taken gold and bronze, respectively, in the 50-meter freestyle), and run back out on deck for the 4 × 100-meter medley relay. David made his way down from the stands—he had no illusions about how I was feeling—but I didn't have time to talk. I dashed over to the warm-down pool, swam half my usual distance, did three quick resistance stretches with Anne and Steve, pulled on my dress sweats, and marched out to the podium to receive my silver medal.

During "Das Deutschlandlied," Britta's German national anthem, I started to cry. I was not crying because I'd lost—my reaction to losing is anger, not tears, and I'm sure plenty of anger flashed across my face. I was crying because I'd come to the end of something. That 24 seconds had consumed nearly two years of my life. I'd swum faster than I ever had before, faster than I'd ever imagined possible even in my prime. Now around my neck hung a silver medal, a complicated prize. My mind started trying to process Britta's margin of victory. I tried to think of something a human being can do in one one-hundredth of a second. I came up empty. You can't breathe. You can't even blink.

I didn't know if my body could handle swimming a fast 100 meters so soon after the 50-meter finals, but Michael and Mark both had confidence in me, so I'd decided to believe in myself as well. Before the medal ceremony, I'd unzipped the torso of my racing suit and rolled the top around my waist. I'd also told Britta and Cate that I didn't intend to be rude but I was going to need to run off the podium, as I had exactly four minutes between the end of the ceremony and the beginning of the medley relay. I spent one of those minutes posing for photographs with Britta and Cate. Then I dashed to the ready room and asked a team manager to zip my LZR suit up. I was the last of the 32 medley-relay swimmers— eight teams, four swimmers on each—to arrive on deck. My cap was still in my hand.

Our lineup in the medley consisted of Natalie Coughlin, who'd won gold in the 100-meter backstroke; Rebecca Soni, who'd won silver in the 100-meter breaststroke; Christine Magnuson, who'd won silver in the 100-meter butterfly; and me. Natalie got off to a great start, with her amazing underwater backstroke kick. At the touch, she handed Rebecca a .39-second lead, but Rebecca had the impossible task of holding off the world-record holder in the 100-meter breaststroke, Leisel Jones of Australia. Rebecca split her fastest time ever, but when she returned to the wall and Christine dove in, we were nearly a second behind. Christine made up a little ground on butterfly. At my start we were trailing the Australians by .87 seconds. Next to me, in lane four, was Libby Trickett, the only person in the world ever to have swum a faster 100-meter relay split than me. She'd gone 52.34 seconds in the 4 × 100-meter relay; I'd gone 52.44 seconds.

Right from my dive I focused on getting up close to our shared lane line so I could ride Libby Trickett's wave. Swimmers don't draft all that often, but it's possible to do, just like on a bike. I was determined to give this race everything I had. Earlier in the Olympics, my American teammate Jason Lezak had pulled off the most amazing anchor leg ever in Olympic swimming, coming from behind to help the men win the 4 × 100-meter freestyle relay, thus preserving Michael Phelps's shot at bringing home eight gold medals. Lezak had swum with so much power and heart, making up a body length against the great French swimmer Alain Bernard in just 50 meters. I wanted to match his performance, though I knew it would be tough. Libby has such amazing turns and such speed underwater, I knew I'd have a hard time closing our gap. I felt really good after my dive, not tired from my 50-meter race, as I'd expected to feel. In the final strokes I was gaining on Libby. I hit the wall so hard that I tore the ligaments in my thumb off the bone.

Once again I looked up at the scoreboard and found I'd come in second. I'd won my third silver medal at this Olympic Games, my twelfth Olympic medal overall. But then I learned my split:

52.27 seconds. I couldn't believe it! I'd swum quicker than either Libby or I ever had before. I hadn't beat her to the wall, but I'd snatched away her record for the fastest 100 meters by a woman in a relay in history.

~ ~ ~ ~ ~

Leaving the Water Cube seemed to take hours. Once I was done racing, my thumb started hurting badly and I was desperate to be home with Tessa, but I had to do another medal ceremony, another drug test, and dozens of interviews. Everyone wanted to know how it felt to lose the biggest race of my life by one one-hundredth of a second. How did it feel to come so close but not win?

I didn't then and I still don't know what a loss like that means. My start had been good, my stroke had been good, my reach had been good, and still I'd come up short. But one thing is certain: I hadn't lost because of my age. Britta Steffen is 17 years younger than I am. If you take one one-hundredth of a second and divide it by 17, you come up with 0.00058 seconds. I didn't lose because my body had been slowing down by 0.00058 seconds per year.

That day I didn't have a lot of insight to offer those reporters. The best I could come up with before I left the Water Cube was "I guess I shouldn't have filed my nails last night."

~ ~ ~ ~ ~

Coming down off the Olympics is always tough. To get to the Games, you push nearly everything beside your sport aside, and it's scary to face what's left when you return. After Sydney in 2000, I feared the emptiness back at home. But now, as a parent, I couldn't wait to return to Tessa. I'd barely seen her in seven weeks.

I arrived home from Beijing, after a 15-hour trip, at 11:30 at night. Tessa was sleeping, of course. I walked into her dark room and sat on her bed. She was out of a crib now, and she looked so small on her full mattress. Next to her, as always, was JoJo, her stuffed dog, and over her head hung a framed copy of the article from the South Florida *Sun-Sentinel* that had been published on May 14, 2006, just about a month after her birth. "She has my fins, that's for sure ... big feet and long hands and long fingers," I'd told Sharon Robb, the reporter who'd come to write about my swimming in Michael's Mother's Day Masters swim meet. Along with the text is a picture of me, holding Tessa, who's a week and a half old and looks like a squishy little peanut. Back then I'd thought my fastest swimming days were over. I'd told the reporter, "If I look at it realistically, I can't do the times I did when I was 33." I'd been wrong.

That night Tessa was sleeping facedown, with her knees tucked under her tummy and her butt straight up in the air. I snuggled with her a moment and kissed her on the head. Then in the morning, not realizing I was home, Tessa called out, "Mori," the name of the nanny who'd been living in the house and taking care of Tessa while David, my mother, and I were all in Beijing. That was painful, I have to admit. As many working mothers can tell you, when a child calls out reflexively for the nanny, you feel a jab to the heart.

But before Tessa even lifted her head, I made this secret sound we have together. It sounds like someone calling a cat. When Tessa hears it, she always knows I'm around.

"Pssst pssst," I said as I ran toward Tessa's door.

She shot off her bed and into my arms. I was so happy to be back.

Tessa's normally not the cuddliest kid—she's too busy for that— but that morning we just lay there, holding each other for a long while, nestled into that perpetual present in which young children live. The Olympics were still going on in China, but I had no regrets about missing the end. I was exactly where I wanted to be. Tessa and I had plastic cars to ride in the driveway. We had a lunchbox to pick out before she started preschool. We had Elmo stories to read.

It's amazing how quickly life returned to normal. I had dozens of errands to run, a mountain of mail had piled up, and I also needed to see Dr. Chalal, my orthopedic surgeon, to discuss my thumb injury and my ongoing shoulder pain. That cortisone shot back in June had helped me through Olympic Trials, but the pain had flared up again in Beijing. Now an MRI showed bone spurs sprouting inside my shoulder joint. So a week after returning home, Chalal performed an "arthroscopic distal clavicle resection"; in other words, he surgically cleaned out my ball-and-socket joint.

Meanwhile Michael, whom I'd last seen when we were working on my starts at Trials, was still at the National Institutes of Health. His health was less precarious than it had been during training camp. He finally returned to Florida two weeks after I arrived home, and I immediately drove over to his house. A full beard covered his face and he could barely get up to say hello. I broke down and cried when I saw him. After we finished hugging, I handed him my medals. I felt they were partly his. We'd talked every day, and I knew he was very sick, but it was still hard to see the guy who'd believed in me looking so weak and gray. The ATG immunosuppressant therapy, which had caused Michael to spike that high fever, had been at least partially successful, but Michael's prognosis remained unclear. He still needed blood transfusions (for the platelets and other blood cells) every few days. His herniated disc could not yet be fixed. Doctors hoped to do a bone-marrow transplant, but even after testing Michael's sister in Germany, they had not found a match.

Like the rest of the world, I'd assumed that after the 2008 Olympics I'd be finished forever with competitive swimming. I was an old hand at retiring from the sport by then. Besides, winning three medals at age 41 had seemed like such an outrageous pushing of age limits, not even I was audacious enough to imagine more. Of course, I intended to stay in great physical shape. I started working out again in the gym as soon as I returned from Beijing. But after my shoulder surgery I couldn't be in the water for two weeks, so it was nearly a month after my last race in Beijing when I finally stuffed my practice suit and goggles into my swim bag again and drove to the Coral Springs pool.

Michael wasn't on the pool deck, which was hard for me. None of my Coral Springs teammates were around. Still, that old plain of cement felt like home. I folded my clothes and put them on the bench. I placed my water bottle under my starting block and I dove in. Once again I felt that ultimate state of transition, my feet no longer on the ground, my hands not yet in the water. I didn't have any expectations for my swim. I knew I still needed to treat my shoulder gingerly, so I just kept my arms by my sides and dolphin-kicked underwater on my back, looking up at the blue and white flags strung over the pool and the late-summer sky beyond.

So much had happened since my first swim here—Tessa's birth, my father's death, Michael's illness, and that infuriating one one-hundredth of a second. That day, I told myself I was just swimming for exercise. It had been 20 years since I'd last returned from an Olympics and kept on training. But my narrow loss still ate at me, and that whole swimming-for-exercise-only mind-set faded as quickly as it had when my fellow Masters swimmer Randy Nutt had started racing me in practice two years before.

So I told myself I'd just swim for exercise until the end of December 2008, at which point I'd have the background to swim in the World Championships in Rome in July 2009 if I wanted to compete. That plan lasted only about a week, too. I was getting older every day, like everyone else on the planet, but—knock on wood—at least so far, my age is not slowing me down. My times had been improving right through my last race in Beijing. Did I want to quit? Hell, no. Before walking out to the medal stand after the medley relay, that final race in Beijing, I'd joked with the other swimmers that I was so happy I'd never have to feel that prerace nausea again, or worry that after months and years of training, my body was going to let me down. But just six weeks later, I craved that nausea. I craved the intensity, the focus, the digging down deep to race the fastest swimmers on earth.

I'll be 42 years old when, in the summer of 2009, I fly into Indianapolis, one more time, to compete in Nationals. A few weeks after that, I hope to swim at the World Championships in Rome. I'll be 45 years old in the summer of 2012 when the next summer Olympic Games come around. Who knows if I'll try to make the Olympic team, or if I'll succeed. But wouldn't it be sweet if a six-year-old Tessa came to London and watched her mother win gold?

Acknowledgments

So many people have helped me achieve my dreams—and set them down in print. My deepest gratitude goes out to: Ed, David, my siblings (Mike, Kirk, Rick, Brad and Lara), my step-siblings (Carol, John, and Colleen), Michael Lohberg, Tommie Nichols, Dr. Kantor, the Richards, Anne Tierney, Steve Sierra, Chris Jackson, Evan Morgenstein, all my teammates on the Coral Springs Swim Club, Andy O'Brien, Dr. Joe Chalal, MB, Bruno Darzi, Jonathan Gellert, Selina Dunworth, Mark Schubert, Terry Palma, Randy Reese, Skip Foster, Richard Quick, Les Unger, Rowdy Gaines, JF, Dick Ebersol and NBC Sports, Dr. Zafran, Bethesda Outpatient Surgery Center, Maura Hertzog, Mori Suarez, Curtis Bell, Steve Dischiavi, Bernard McCue, Sue Carswell, the Monaghans, SMI, Speedo, Toyota, USA Swimming, USADA, Travis Tygart, Living Fuel, Fitness Nutrition Aminos, Barbara Protzman, Nicole Haislett-Bacher, Paige Zemina-Northcutt, Ginger Southall, Jack Barnathan, Robert Weir, Darlene Bible, Kerry and Dan O'Mahoney, James Bauman, Pam Barone, Ilena Silverman, Catherine Saint Lewis, Dan Duane, Kris Dahl, and Stacy Creamer.